W9-BZV-765

Let the Redeemed of the Lord Say So!

Expressing Your Faith Through Witnessing

H. Eddie Fox
George E. Morris

Abingdon Press
Nashville

LET THE REDEEMED OF THE LORD SAY SO!
Expressing Your Faith Through Witnessing

Copyright © 1991 by Abingdon Press

All rights reserved.

No part of this work may be reproduced or transmitted in any form or by any means, electronic or mechanical, including photocopying and recording, or by any information storage or retrieval system, except as may be expressly permitted by the 1976 Copyright Act or in writing from the publisher. Requests for permission should be addressed in writing to Abingdon Press, 201 Eighth Avenue South, Nashville, TN 37203.

This book is printed on recycled, acid-free paper.

Library of Congress Cataloging-in-Publication Data

Fox, H. Eddie.
    Let the redeemed of the Lord say so : expressing your faith through witnessing / H. Eddie Fox, George E. Morris.
        p.   cm.
    Includes bibliographical references.
    ISBN 0-687-21380-0
    1. Witness bearing (Christianity)   2. Evangelistic work.
I. Morris, George E., 1935-   . II. Title.
BV4520.F685   1991
248'.5—dc20
                                                           91-17857
                                                           CIP

All scripture quotations, unless otherwise noted, are from the New Revised Standard Version of the Bible, copyright 1989 by the Division of Christian Education of the National Council of the Churches of Christ in the USA.

Scripture quoted from *The New English Bible* copyright The Delegates of the Oxford University Press and The Syndics of the Cambridge University Press 1961, 1970. Reprinted by permission.

Scripture quoted from the *New American Standard Bible*, copyright The Lockman Foundation 1960, 1962, 1968, 1971, 1972, 1973, 1975, 1977.

Quotations marked KJV are from the *King James Version of the Bible*.

Scripture quoted from *The Revised English Bible* copyright Oxford University Press and Cambridge University Press 1989.

MANUFACTURED IN THE UNITED STATES OF AMERICA

Dedicated to

JOE HALE

Ambassador of Jesus Christ

to the *whole* world

Foreword

As the world approaches the end of this millennium
there is a quickening of questions about where
humankind has travelled so far and, more important-
ly, where we are to go in the future. In such a setting it
is hardly surprising that many Christians around the world
are talking about a Decade of Evangelisation. If the world
family is asking big questions about its past and its future,
then surely the Christian gospel should be at the centre of
that discussion.

The scale of that task is so enormous, however, that we
must realise that it can never be achieved by relying solely on
evangelistic preachers and large compaigns, necessary as
those are and will continue to be. We can only reach the
whole world population through the witness of every
Christian, wherever God has placed her or him. It is the
personal witness of the family member in the home, or the
colleague at work, or the neighbour in the road, or the friend
at the place of leisure which enables others to see that the
gospel is for them also. People will only hear what that
message is if the redeemed of the Lord say so.

The major problem is that so many members of our
churches don't really believe that such a plan involves them!
They're very modest about the quality of their lives, or about
the limits of their knowledge, or about the shortage of
adequate vocabulary. What many of us need is to discover,
along with others, that it is precisely people like us who are
not self-confident but rather modest about ourselves, whom
God has used from the beginning. As we learn to grasp the
fundamentals of our faith and the way they relate to people's

needs, we may begin to believe that we might be of use. If we can then see ways in which people have managed to make a spoken witness, we can get a glimpse of what the way forward might be for ourselves. It isn't a matter of learning set techniques which ensure "success." It's much more about gaining confidence in the faith we have, and in the Lord who wishes to use us.

When it comes to helping Christians towards that mixture of quiet confidence and commitment to witness, I know of no other pair of teachers anywhere in the world who have more insight or skill than H. Eddie Fox and George E. Morris. They both learned the art of witnessing in tough areas of their homeland. They have built on that beginning with sound theological education and pastoral experience. Recently both have been teaching and learning about witness on the world scene, particularly in connection with the World Evangelism Committee and the World Evangelism Institute based at Candler School of Theology, Emory University, Atlanta. Through these experiences they have not only taught and influenced many around the world, they have also learned from people in different cultural contexts. All of their richness they now make available to us.

Since there are so many texts on evangelism today, however, one does need to explain the publishing of yet another! Why is this book likely to be outstanding in the help it offers to readers? I offer the following answers to that question.

First, it is personal. It never strays away from the realities of everyday life. It is not a set of theories struggling for a foundation. It begins with how life is and sees the message of the gospel in that light.

Then, it's biblical. We are never far away from the teaching of Jesus or the ideas of Paul, or the testimony of the other biblical writers. We see in this book how scripture and daily life are meant to relate. As you work through these pages you will learn a great deal about the faith itself as well as about how to share it.

In the third place, it shows it's Methodist base. That need not inhibit non-Methodists from using it! But these men are Methodist preachers and teachers, so you'd expect it to show! In this two-hundredth year since John Wesley's death, it is appropriate to have a book which shares his passion "to offer them Christ."

It's also a manageable book. The reader doesn't feel overwhelmed by it, or "talked down to" by it. You feel that you could get on with these two writers if they were to walk into your home. Since they have both at various times walked into mine, I can tell you that this is a true judgement.

I commend this book whole-heartedly, for individual reading and for use in training classes and in seminary and college courses. People will grow spiritually as they use it, and the church will grow in numbers as we all put it into practice. If we believe in our gospel, then, "Let the people of the Lord say so!" I'm grateful that this book will help us to do so.

Donald English, President
World Methodist Council

Acknowledgments

Writing a book is an exciting, demanding, and challenging task. This is the second time we have written a book together in order to share our deep convictions. It is not easy to co-author a book. It requires great introspection about the clear essentials we hold in the faith. Writing together means that both authors concur on the many issues raised in the text. Our pilgrimage has required a mutual commitment to the faith, to one another, and to the mission and ministry of the church. Over a period of many months we have engaged in extensive dialogue, research, and prayer.

This process has resulted in the deepening of our friendship and in our total commitment to Jesus Christ. We have been driven by our passion to evangelize the good news of Jesus Christ to the whole world. This is a *kairos* time in the life of the church for world evangelization. At no other time in our lives have we felt a greater joy and sense of urgency in sharing the faith through preaching and testifying.

Both authors assume responsibility for the entire text. We are tremendously indebted to a host of people. We were shaped by families, friends, and pastors in our early Christian journey. It is impossible to name the entire cloud of witnesses that surround us in our ministry, but we certainly must mention the following people: Carl Bates, Herndon Shepherd, Ray Hargraves, Joe Hale, Larry Lacour, O. Dean Martin, George Outen, Glenn "Tex" Evans, George Hunter, III, Shirley Clement, Maxie Dunnam, Alan Walker, Ed Beck, Donald English and, of course, Harry Denman. In addition, teachers and colleagues have greatly contributed to our understanding of communicating the gospel: John Killinger, Fred Craddock, Ron Sleeth and Leander Keck. We must also express appreciation to Mary Hall and Jacque Richardson who aided in the preparation of the manuscript.

Two witnesses in the faith, whom we acknowledge with greatest gratitude, are Mary Nell Fox and Barbara Morris. They, truly, in both word and deed speak as those who are redeemed in the Lord.

It is our deep prayer and abiding hope that the Holy Spirit will use these writings to instruct and inspire the "Redeemed of the Lord to SAY SO!"

H. Eddie Fox
World Director of Evangelism
World Methodist Council

George E. Morris, Director
World Methodist Evangelism Institute
Candler School of Theology
Emory University

Contents

Introduction: Let the Redeemed of the Lord Say So! 13

Part One: A Case for Preaching and Testifying 17

    1. Stating the Case 19
    2. Witnessing Matters 29
    3. Confidence to Speak Out 37

Part Two: Content of Preaching and Testifying 49

    4. The Message of Jesus 51
    5. The Message Goes Forth 65
    6. The Gospel Demands a Response 81

Part Three: The Context for Preaching and Testifying 93

    7. Hearing the People's Cry 95
    8. Organizing the Message 107

Part Four: Communicating the Gospel 119

    9. Inviting Response 121
    10. Methods of Inviting Response 135
    11. Taking the Stand 153

Part Five: Credibility and Courage of the
Witness   *159*

         12.   The Word Becomes Flesh   *161*
         13.   The Courage to Keep On   *169*

Notes   *181*

Suggested Reading   *185*

Appendix   *189*

Let the Redeemed of the Lord Say So!

This book is written on the basis of one clear and powerful conviction: the time is right for the church to put primary emphasis upon verbal witnessing to the gospel of Jesus Christ. We are convinced that preaching and testifying are both the expectation of God and the desperate need in today's world.

Psalm 107 gives expression to this expectation and need. After acknowledging the steadfast and eternal love of God and the praise that wells up in the human heart because of God's redemptive action, the psalmist declares: "Let the redeemed of the Lord say so. . . ." (Ps. 107:2).

This declaration of the Psalmist desperately needs to be heard in today's church. In recent history we have moved through a period in which some church leaders in parts of the world have tended to emphasize doing the deeds of the gospel almost at the expense of verbal witnessing. In fact, there were those who went so far as to call for a moratorium on all speech. Now we do not wish to insinuate that deeds are unimportant. In our earlier book, *Faith-Sharing*, we made a strong case for the necessity of holding word and deed in a delicate balance. In that book we contend and continue to believe that the gospel is, by its very nature, both *visible* and *verbal*.

However, our travels across North America and in many countries of the world and our firsthand association with

Christian sisters and brothers convince us that this is the *kairos* moment. The time is right to put primary emphasis on speaking out for the Lord!

The Christian community has tended to shy away from the clear biblical mandate of bearing witness through preaching and testimony. It is often easier to do the deed of the gospel than to name the name of Jesus Christ. We suspect that the reason for this is related to that important incarnational word **vulnerability**. A human is never more vulnerable than when he or she raises to speech the deepest thoughts, commitments, and desires of life. In some ways the frenzied activities of church work can be a means of avoiding the risky business of speaking for the Lord.

It is possible to do "church work" with the extremities of one's body. But, when one talks about one's relationship with God, one is bringing that up from the deepest recesses of one's being. At that point a person is always vulnerable. It may be that the church's reluctance to give verbal witness is an attempt on the part of the church to render itself increasingly invulnerable. There was once an era in the church's life when peachers were trained not to include any of their inner faith or struggle in their presentations of the gospel.

The psalmist shouts "Let the redeemed of the Lord say so. . . ." He proceeds to illustrate the breadth and depth of redemption. He speaks of those who wander in "desert wastes finding no way to an inhabited town." Lost and lonely, these persons cry to the Lord in their distress and the Lord leads them "by a straight way" to a city in which they can now live (Ps. 107:4-9).

In our times these words echo the experiences of millions whose lives were like a desert waste until they discovered the Lord and the vitality of the Christian community. These persons must take the stand and give witness to their redemption (Ps. 107:10-16). The redeemed of the Lord *must* say so.

There are countless others in the church who once sat in darkness and bondage because they flouted the purposes of the living God. However, they cried to the Lord at midnight and God heard them. God showed steadfast love by freeing them and bringing them from darkness to light. The time has come for these Christians to find their voice and tell of the marvelous work of God's grace in their lives. The redeemed of the Lord must say so (Ps. 107:10-16)!

Many Christians who once knew the pain of brokenness of heart, body, and soul have experienced the "balm in Gilead that heals the sin-sick soul." These people must speak out to a world which longs for a word of healing and wholeness. The redeemed of the Lord must *say* so (Ps. 107:17-22)!

Other people in the church could tell of their lives at "wit's end" (Ps. 107:27). They found themselves on a merry-go-round of activity in their work. Being tossed to and fro, they reeled and staggered like drunken people. However, they looked to the Lord who brought them out of their distress and guided them through the storms of life (Ps. 107:23-32). The time has come for the *redeemed* of the *Lord* to *say* so!

In our ministry we have discovered countless vital, dynamic Christians who have experienced a genuine work of God in their lives. But they have not always been encouraged to speak out. To the contrary, they have been admonished, often by default, to remain silent. On the other hand, we know the enormous power unleashed when Christians are willing to risk vulnerability, to take the stand and testify to their faith in the Lord Jesus Christ.

As we move through the final decade of this century and into the next millennium, it is our conviction that God intends to gather "in from the lands, from the east and from the west, from the north and from the south" millions of new Christians. We believe that we are already well into a new movement of the Holy Spirit across the face of the earth. If our churches are to be part of this vital movement of the

Spirit, we must encourage and train our people to **speak up** and **speak out**.

The world is hungry for the message of Jesus Christ. Emilio Castro believes that the absolute central task of the church is that of telling the story of Jesus. He states, "The story of Jesus Christ is the real novelty, the new breakthrough. In the 1990's, like the apostle Paul we must be ready to *say* 'For I decided to know nothing among you except Jesus Christ, and him crucified'" (1 Cor. 2:2).[1]

This book, a sequel to *Faith-Sharing*, without apology, puts emphasis on the essential necessity of preaching and testifying of the good news of Jesus Christ. We dare to join our voices with that of the psalmist and cry out to the church: LET THE REDEEMED OF THE LORD SAY SO!

Part One

A Case for Preaching and Testifying

Chapter One

Stating the Case

A young woman, struggling with her call to witness, said, "For anyone to stand up and attempt to speak in the name of God is the height of presumption." She is correct, but that is exactly what pastors and lay speakers do week after week and that is exactly what we have been called to do. Why are we so presumptuous? It is a rather audacious thing to do! Who do we think we are? At the outset it is important that we give attention to the reasons why preaching and giving testimony have always been a part of the Christian movement.

Why Preaching and Testifying

1. We preach and testify because Jesus, our Lord, preached and testified. Matthew's Gospel tells us that at the dawning of Jesus' Galilean ministry and upon learning of John's arrest, "From that time Jesus began to proclaim, 'Repent, for the kingdom of heaven has come near'" (Matt. 4:17). According to Luke, Jesus announced his public ministry at Nazareth by saying: "The Spirit of the Lord is upon me, because he has anointed me to bring good news to the poor. He has sent me to proclaim release to the captives and recovery of sight to the blind, to let the oppressed go free, to proclaim the year of the Lord's favor" (Luke 4:18-19). Whatever else Jesus was, he was a "faithful witness" (Rev. 1:5).

Now it would be wrong to insinuate that preaching and
testimony are the only ways of communicating the gospel.
However, it would be equally incorrect to insinuate that
preaching and testimony played a relatively unimportant role
in the ministry of Jesus. Jesus never hesitated to speak out! To
Nicodemus, a religious official, he declared, "We speak of
what we know and testify to what we have seen" (John 3:11).
Jesus, our Lord, *proclaimed* the good news.

2. We preach and give testimony because Jesus has
commanded us to do so. In Mark's Gospel, as a prelude to our
Lord's Ascension, and after rebuking his disciples for their
incredulity and dullness, Jesus says, "Go into all the world
and proclaim the good news to the whole creation" (Mark
16:15). This is the more-than-cosmic framework in which we
are called to communicate the gospel. Not only the whole
world but the whole creation needs to receive the gospel.
What an affirmation of the universal nature of the gospel! It is
not merely for the human community, but it has a liberating
and redeeming word for all creation.

Moreover, as the early church took root and began to grow,
it did so upon the basis of fervent preaching and testimony. In
Peter's address in Acts 10:42, he says, "He commanded us to
preach to the people and to testify that he is the one ordained
by God." According to this text, Jesus is admonishing his
followers to *preach* and *testify*. In addition, Jesus is saying
that *he* is the content of the good news of the gospel. Thus, we
can understand why Paul warns young Timothy, "Do not be
ashamed, then, of the testimony about our Lord or of me his
prisoner, but join with me in suffering for the gospel, relying
on the power of God, who saved us and called us with a holy
calling, not according to our works but according to his own
purpose and grace" (2 Tim. 1:8-9*a*). To fail to give testimony
is symptomatic of being ashamed of the gospel. And to be
ashamed of the gospel is to be ashamed of the Christ who has
called us with a holy calling.

Numerous reasons are given for the current decline of oldline denominations. These reasons are often supported by sociological studies and demographic analyses. Such studies and analyses are necessary and helpful, but do not give the basic reason for decline—the reason being that too many Christians are ashamed of the testimony about our Lord. The fact is, these oldline church members are even reluctant to invite their neighbors to church, let alone declare the good news of the gospel.[1] The scriptures insist that in our hearts we must "sanctify Christ as Lord" and always be ready to make our defense to anyone who demands an accounting for the hope that is in us (1 Pet. 3:15). It is our hope that God will use this book to help us "sanctify Christ as Lord," and "rekindle the gift of God" that will move preachers and lay-speakers beyond "a spirit of cowardice" to a "spirit of power and of love and of "self-discipline" (2 Tim. 1:6-7). Fundamentally, the growth of the church in every respect depends on courageous preaching and testimony, and we accept this mandate because Jesus, our Lord, has given it.

It is interesting to note the frequent references to preaching and testifying in the New Testament. Any serious treatment of the New Testament will show that preaching and giving testimony are God's primary ways of communicating the gospel. Because of this, William Barclay claims that "preaching was the main means of conversion in the early church."[2] And Michael Green insists that the earliest Christians went everywhere "gossiping the Gospel."[3] Once we acknowledge these important truths, it is easier to understand why Paul said, "Woe to me if I do not proclaim the gospel!" (1 Cor. 9:16) We are confident that Paul wondered about his presumptuous vocation, for in 1 Cor. 1:21 he alludes to the "foolishness of our proclamation." Nevertheless, as his letter to Titus clearly states, Paul is confident that God "revealed his word through the proclamation" (Titus 1:3). Thus, at the outset we affirm that we preach and give testimony because our Lord was a faithful witness and has commanded us to do the same.

3. Preaching and testifying make possible an encounter with Christ. The primary purpose of preaching or testimony is to lift up Christ. Jesus said, "And I, when I am lifted up from the earth, will draw all people to myself." (John 12:32) Preaching or testifying that lifts up Christ makes possible an encounter with Christ. This is why preaching and testimony are such powerful forms of communication.

Jesus Christ is both the subject and object of preaching and testimony, just as he is the very center of the church's life. The New Testament portrays the church as a community of believers gathered around Jesus (Matt. 18:15-20; Acts 2:42; Eph. 4:1-16; Phil. 2:1-11). One of the most succinct definitions of the church can be found in Matthew's Gospel: "For where two or three are gathered in my name, I am there among them" (18:20). The church has its beginning when two or three people come together "in the name of Jesus."

The church is a community of people gathered around Jesus, committed to him, worshiping him, testifying to him and ready to serve his kingdom in the world. According to Howard Snyder, "People gathered around Jesus is the irreducible minimum of the church."[4] Thus Jesus Christ, the proclaimer par excellence, has commanded us to preach and give testimony because this enables people to experience his living presence.

4. We presume to preach and testify because they are closely linked with Christian education. In the New Testament Jesus is viewed as a rabbi or teacher. John's Gospel presents him as the teacher without peer (John 3:2; 13:13). Is it any wonder that large sections of the Gospels are devoted to the *teachings* of Jesus? His sermon on the mount could be called his *teaching* on the mount. In the tradition of Moses he climbs a mountain, gathers his disciples, and teaches in the rabbinic style. In the early development of the church we see how Paul taught in synagogues and homes (Acts 18:4-7; 19:8-9). Teaching is referred to as an "office" in several New Testament writings (1 Cor. 12:28-29; Eph. 4:11; 1 Tim. 4:6, 11, 16; 6:2-3).

Certainly, those who preach and testify would do well to emulate the New Testament model of ministry. It is especially interesting to note how closely preaching, testimony, and teaching are linked. In the New Testament, when teaching is mentioned, preaching or testimony usually follows in the next breath. Matthew reports that Jesus "went throughout Galilee teaching in their synagogues and preaching the good news of the kingdom and curing every disease" (Matt. 4:23). In the instruction given by Paul to Timothy (1 Tim. 4:13; 5:17), we see that preaching means both public proclamation of the gospel to unbelievers, and teaching the gospel to believers as part of regular worship. God, through the power of the Holy Spirit, can give to all believers the freedom and ability to read the Bible and understand the gospel. However, the Holy Spirit gives gifts to believers for the ministry of preaching, testimony, and teaching (1 Cor. 12:28; Acts 6:2; Eph. 4:11). The church must continue to seek to identify and encourage members who have these gifts.

Paul says to Timothy in 2 Timothy 4:1-5:

> In the presence of God and of Christ Jesus, who is to judge the living and the dead, and in view of his appearing and his kingdom, I solemnly urge you: proclaim the message; be persistent whether the time is favorable or unfavorable; convince, rebuke, and encourage, with the utmost patience in teaching. For the time is coming when people will not put up with sound doctrine, but having itching ears, they will accumulate for themselves teachers to suit their own desires, and will turn away from listening to the truth and wander away to myths. As for you, always be sober, endure suffering, do the work of an evangelist, carry out your ministry fully.

In few New Testament passages are the duties of the preacher-testifier more clearly set out than in this one. After outlining the critical times in which Timothy is to fulfill his vocation, Paul charges Timothy to fulfill his calling and do his duty as if he were doing it in the presence of God and of Jesus Christ. Paul wants Timothy to understand that his essential function is to preach and teach the Word of God and to bear witness incessantly whether the occasion is favorable or not, or whether people will listen and respond or not. According to Paul, Timothy is to preach, testify, and teach in a convincing manner, with a note of prophetic rebuke, and he is to appeal to people to respond in repentance and in faith.

The preceding passage gives evidence of the close ties between preaching, testimony, and Christian education. In his book, *Apostolic Preaching and Its Development*,[5] C. H. Dodd made a sharp distinction between preaching and teaching. Dodd attempted to show that apostolic preaching focused on the birth, death, burial, resurrection, exaltation and return of Jesus, while teaching focused on ethical instruction and exhortation. Unfortunately, Dodd's observations tended to force a dichotomy between preaching, testimony, and Christian education.

However, we now realize that Dodd's artificial division cannot be fully supported by New Testament evidence.[6] For instance, we know that much teaching in the early church was aimed not at believers but at anyone who would listen. Moreover, we now know that teaching occurred in various places—synagogues, the temple, hilltops, houses, etc. We now know that the words *testifying*, *preaching*, and *teaching* were sometimes used interchangeably and that a close link was forged between them in the New Testament. The importance of this linkage needs to be reaffirmed. More and more attention needs to be given to adult teaching and discipling. Ordained preachers, local preachers, lay speakers, and Sunday school teachers—all Christians—must give more attention to this need. We need to understand that our best proclamation is also our most effective teaching, and our best teaching often results in a profound communication of the gospel.

5. Preaching and testifying are primary ways through which the church gives witness. The word *witness* derives from the Greek root *martus* or *martureo*. From these words we derive our English word *martyr*. The word *witness* and its cognates appear over two hundred times in the New Testament. The origin of the word is deeply rooted in the Old Testament concept of justice and centers in the lawsuit or controversy themes in the legal assemblies of the Old Testament. The word also appears frequently in the Greek law courts. Wherever there is an attempt to establish *facts*, the Greeks used the word *witness* to denote "giving evidence." Thus, you give evidence in order to present the truth. The New Testament usage of the word rests squarely upon the Old Testament legal assembly with points of similarity to the Greek law courts.

Emphasis upon Witness

According to Allison Trites, the word *witness* in its New Testament usage stresses two important points. *First*, it stresses the historical foundations of Christianity. The use of the word *witness* proves that the mission of the early church was a *public* mission. Nothing was done in secret. To the contrary, there is repeated emphasis on historical *facts*, and these facts are attested to by reliable witnesses. This greatly strengthens the case for Christian truth.

Second, the New Testament emphasis on witness stresses the importance of the place of apologetics in a skeptical age. Trites maintains that our age is similar to the New Testament world in that both worlds are extremely skeptical. Both require Christians to give a reason for the hope that is in us. In a skeptical environment a brief must be presented,

arguments must be advanced, and witnesses brought forward
if the case for Christianity is to be given a proper hearing.[7]

Preaching, testifying and witnessing are closely linked, and
this linkage has powerful implications for contemporary
preachers and lay witnesses. Throughout the history of the
church loyalty to profound convictions and witnessing to
those convictions has led to persecution and suffering. The
first chapter of Revelation states: "I, John, your brother who
shares with you in Jesus the persecution and the kingdom and
the patient endurance, was on the island called Patmos
because of the word of God and the testimony of Jesus" (1:9).
Giving faithful testimony has often led to suffering and
imprisonment. This is still true today, especially where
Christians live under oppressive regimes.

This emphasis also implies that witnesses are passionately
involved in the case they seek to present. They have been
apprehended by it and therefore have an inner compulsion to
plead its merits with others. They echo the words of the
prophet: "Within me there is something like a burning fire
shut up in my bones; I am weary with holding it in, and I
cannot" (Jer. 20:9). The first-century Christian witnesses
declared, "We cannot keep from speaking about what we
have seen and heard" (Acts 4:20).

Once the witness has seen, heard, beheld or perceived an
event the witness then is compelled to testify. Pope Paul VI
boldly stated, "It is unthinkable that a person should accept
Christ and give himself to the kingdom without becoming a
person who bears witness to it and proclaims it in his turn."[8]
Here we see the two-sided rhythm of Christian witness. On
the one hand, witness involves perceiving something as an
active observer. On the other hand, witness means saying
something. It means making others aware. As Thomas G.
Long observes, witness in the first place means to perceive or
behold an event. Witness in the second sense means to testify
to that event, to speak out![9]

This implies that the ones who preach or testify are held accountable for the truthfulness of their witness. Perjury was, and still is, a serious offense. Thus, those of us who preach and testify are driven back to the scriptures as the test of the validity of our witness. We must be faithful not only to the bare facts of the gospel, but also to its meaning and how that meaning has transformed our lives. We must speak of the birth, life, death, and resurrection of Jesus in such a way that the intrinsic divine significance of these events is brought to light.

6. We presume to preach and testify because they are a means of initiating the hearer into the reign of God. The intention of preaching and testifying must always be that of announcing the kingdom of God. Thus, preaching and testimony are not ends in themselves but means toward a greater end—the reign of God. The aim of preaching and testimony is to lift up Christ in such a way that all people will be drawn to God and submit to the supreme authority of Jesus, sanctify Christ as Lord, and become free for the kingdom. It follows that preaching and testifying are of vital significance because the kingdom is of vital significance. They are a means of winning people to Jesus and his kingdom.

Problems come when preaching is made an end in itself and when testifying is merely an autobiographical statement unrelated to the message of the kingdom. Jesus has told us that the central focus of the church's message is the kingdom of God—the justice, mercy, and faithfulness of that kingdom (Matt. 6:33; 13:23; 23:23; Luke 11:42). Christians are to pray constantly and expectantly that God's kingdom may come, meaning that God's *will* be done on earth as it is in heaven (Matt. 6:10). Witnessing that fails to be grounded in the message of the kingdom cannot be said to be Christian. Preaching and testifying must be done with the express purpose of initiating persons into the reign of God. This is the "norming norm" of gospel communication and every other purpose must be judged in the light of this supreme purpose. What makes preaching, teaching, and testifying "Christian" is that these actions are a part of a process that has as its goal the initiating of people into the kingdom of God.

This process will involve the proclamation of the good news of the kingdom; the call to repentance and faith in Jesus Christ; patient teaching in which the person can be grounded in Christian faith and incorporated into the fellowship of the church; the equipping of each Christian to be an agent of the kingdom in the world and the encouragement to use his or her gifts to the fullest.

Thus, we presume to preach and testify because Jesus our Lord was a faithful witness and he commanded us to preach and testify. We presume to preach and testify because this makes possible an encounter with Christ. Moreover, Christian education is always included in Christian witnessing. We preach and testify because they are the primary means of Christian witness. Finally, we preach and testify because God has ordained that these are a means by which persons are initiated into the kingdom of God. Is it any wonder that the Bible says, "Let the redeemed of the Lord say so"?

Chapter Two

Witnessing
Matters

I t is crucial that we now set forth our understanding of
what preaching and testifying mean, why they are
important, how they relate to the community of faith,
and the source of power that makes them possible. By
the terms *preaching* and *testifying* we mean:

> To proclaim the biography of the deeds of God in terms
> of one's autobiography with the hope that persons,
> enabled by the power of the Holy Spirit, respond to
> God's act of forgiveness in Jesus Christ, in repentance
> and faith, and live out the new life in faithfulness to the
> kingdom of God.

Each phrase in this definition is a key to understanding these
two terms, and each will be discussed in depth in succeeding
chapters.

From this definition it is obvious that preaching and
testifying matter! When a person is preaching or testifying to
the good news of Jesus Christ, there is nothing more important.
Dr. William E. Sangster wrote, "On one's way to preach the
gospel the most modest person may whisper, 'Nothing more
important will happen in this town this week than the work I am
doing now!'"[10] God has chosen to be revealed and to be made
known through the verbal witness to the gospel.

Probably no task in ministry makes a person as nervous as daring to take the stand and testify to the good news of what God has done for the world. For many years both of us have traveled across the world and talked with pastors and lay leaders about their ministries. It is a difficult and sensitive task to talk with persons about their witnessing because there is no place in the ministry of the church in which one becomes more nervous or uptight than in verbalizing the gospel. Our personal experience confirms this. If you criticize our preaching and testifying, please do it gently. Many lay witnesses or preachers have known the agony of having a friend say, "I'm not quite sure the people got the message today." That's about as much as we can take! The friend is actually saying, "You really messed up today." Fortunately, the friend knows that we could never endure such criticism. It is simply too much to bear.

Why this level of sensitivity regarding our attempts to verbalize the gospel? There is something about preaching and testifying (choosing to raise profound convictions to the level of speech and utterance) which makes us vulnerable. When we witness, we open our lives to others. This is risky, yet, we dare to do it. After all, *the redeemed of the Lord must say so.*

Witnessing Is God's Idea

God's self is revealed through the proclamation of the Word. We testify in the name of God who chose to be known to all creation through Jesus Christ. As Jesus said, "I testify on my behalf, and the Father who sent me testifies on my behalf" (John 8:18). All of this is God's idea. It is not the desire of God that anyone should live in darkness or that anyone should perish, but rather that all should come to repentance (2 Pet. 3:9).

Some time ago there was an interesting story about whales that were trapped in the ice off the coast of Alaska. They swam in the cool waters so long that they missed the last plane to

Hawaii! They were completely enclosed by the deepening ice. Some people saw their plight and tried to rescue them by sawing through the ice, but they were unsuccessful and called for additional help. The United States Navy sent in a ship to rescue the whales. That, too, failed. Finally, a Soviet ice-breaker was asked to plow through the ice allowing the whales to swim out into the open sea. Before the Russian ship started its work, a United States of America flag was raised on its mast. People, especially the Press Corps, could hardly believe it! Here was a USA flag on a Russian ship! A whale was used to bring two countries, often at odds with each other, together for the sake of rescue.

We remember another story about a whale, the story of Jonah. It is remarkable that this story, with its powerful message, was included in the canon of the Bible. There are some who would prefer to remove it. They imagine that God is interested only in them and their kind of people. However, when one gets to the heart of the Jonah story, one discovers two fundamental truths. First, it was not Jonah's idea to go to Nineveh. Second, it was not the Ninevites' idea to hear about God; that was God's idea.

It seems that God is forever calling reluctant missionaries. John Wesley writes that he went "rather unwillingly" to a prayer meeting on Aldersgate Street. Yet, it was at this prayer meeting that a new assurance of God's forgiveness came to him. Furthermore, Wesley reluctantly decided to become even "more vile" and venture into field or open air preaching and witnessing. Previously, he thought the "saving of souls almost a sin if it had not been done in church."[11] Nevertheless, on April 2, 1739, he recorded one of the most significant decisions in his entire ministry:

> At four in the afternoon I submitted to be more vile, and proclaimed in the highways the glad tidings of salvation, speaking from a *little eminence* [italics added] in a ground adjoining to the city to about three thousand people.[12]

John Wesley was very reluctant to move outside the comfortable confines of the church. He felt that the gospel witness must not be a huckster. Yet when he stood on that "little eminence" in the ground, he saw a new vision of the world. He now could see farther and clearer than he had ever seen.

Two of the great biblical models are Moses and Jesus: Moses and the burning bush on Mount Sinai, Jesus and the disciples on the Mount of Transfiguration. Moses, Jesus and the disciples, as well as Wesley, experienced an alteration of perspective while on a mountain. Mountains, even small mountains such as an "eminence in the ground," have a way of doing that for people. As David Martin reminds us, "Mountains increase the range of vision by providing a new angle unblocking the doors of perception."[13]

Later in his ministry, Wesley reluctantly made the decision to use lay persons in preaching the gospel. For a long time he resisted taking what he thought was a radical step. In each of these well-documented cases, Wesley was moved by the fact that he followed a God who desires to be known, loved, and worshiped. On the first Sunday in the open air (April 8, 1739) he proclaimed the gospel to five thousand people and he wrote the following:

> I stood and cried in the "name of the Lord." If anyone thirst, let him come unto me and drink. He that believeth on me, as the scripture hath said, out of his belly shall flow rivers of living water.[14]

In each of these decisions, so critical in the history of the Methodist Movement, Wesley was always propelled by the call of God.

The message of the Book of Jonah proclaims it was God's idea that the people of Nineveh hear the word of the Lord. The message is clear. The deepest, darkest, dampest, dreariest, and most desolate place—the belly of a whale in the depths of the sea—does not thwart God's mission. Let no one think for one moment that preaching and testifying are human inventions; they are God's idea. And what an idea!

The Witness Never Stands Alone

Witnessing is a ministry of the community of those who have faith in Jesus, the Christ. In other words, preaching and testifying is a ministry of the church. Those who witness are not freelance artists who simply drift around without any accountability. It is God who calls forth the witness. But it is the church, when it is healthy, that offers encouragement and support, while at the same time holding the witness accountable to the truth of the gospel (Heb. 10:23-25).

The witness never stands alone! In the New Testament, whether it is Simon Peter speaking in the marketplace, Paul preaching in the stadium in Ephesus, or Stephen witnessing to the angry mob, they all make their witness from the base provided from the community of believers. Witnessing is never an individualistic task. Even when John Wesley preached in the open air, he did so as a member of the community of faith. When Donald Soper of London, England, presents the gospel in the open air at Hyde Park, he speaks from a small platform with a sign that reads "The Methodist Church." The message is clear: Donald Soper knows that he is never alone when he takes the stand. The one who testifies never does it in isolation. It is always from within the community of faith that we speak, and it is to the community of believers that we return. Within the community we are continually nurtured, inspired, and challenged to go forth into the world as God's witness.

There is a rhythm between prayer and preaching, communion and communication, teaching and testifying, exposition and exhortation, worship and witnessing. God calls and the community of faith takes responsibility for fulfilling the command of Jesus: "Go into all the world and

proclaim the good news to the whole creation" (Mark 16:15).
But what is the source of power for such a momentous task?

By the Power of the Holy Spirit

We know from our study of scripture, church history, and
our own personal experience that all attempts to witness to
the gospel are bound to fail without the invigorating power of
the Holy Spirit. The Holy Spirit is the primary witness.
Scripture teaches that the Holy Spirit "testifies to us" (Heb.
10:15). The Holy Spirit is available, not merely for the
edification of individual believers, but for the empowerment
of the whole church. The Holy Spirit is the breath of the body.
Without the Holy Spirit, the body is breathless, powerless,
and dead. This means no Holy Spirit, no effective witnessing
to the gospel.

Unfortunately, in parts of the church, the Holy Spirit is the
missing note in attempts to preach and testify. This lack of
emphasis on the power and gifts of ministry from the Holy
Spirit is producing a church that is declining or merely
holding its own. Lack of the Holy Spirit produces a church
that is noncontagious, timid, fearful, and without spiritual
and moral energy. Without Pentecost and the power of the
Holy Spirit, the church remains behind closed doors afraid for
its life (Mark 16:8; John 20:19). "But when the Holy Spirit
comes," transformation happens. John Wesley wrote, "The
renewal of the soul, after the image of God . . . can never be
wrought in us except by the power of the Holy Ghost."[15] At
Pentecost, a new vision and power moves into the followers of
Jesus, taking control. The Holy Spirit cleanses the church of
self-centeredness, gives gifts for ministry, and transforms
timid believers into bold witnesses.

We have incredible good news! We have not only been
given a commission, but we have also been given the power to
fulfill the assignment. In the Book of Acts massive emphasis is
given to the invigorating power of the Holy Spirit and the

faith that develops in response to the hearing of the gospel. Therefore, the growth of congregations was not a tribute to human ingenuity and enterprise, but a witness to the truth of the gospel and the prevailing power of the Holy Spirit. People responded to the good news, opened their lives to the power of the Holy Spirit, were overwhelmed with gratitude for God's grace and proceeded to witness with boldness and confidence.

Then, as well as now, it is the power of the Holy Spirit that gives the redeemed the confidence to *say so*! Modern Christians need to bring to the task of witnessing the very best they have in terms of human ingenuity and enterprise. Without Pentecost, however, our own efforts are less than adequate and our confidence evaporates. And as we shall indicate in the next chapter, the confidence to preach and testify is of tremendous importance.

Chapter Three

Confidence to Speak Out

G iving public testimony with an expectation for response presupposes a confidence in God, in the proclaimed Word, and in the act of preaching and testifying. The witness must constantly ask: " Do I expect God to disclose God's self in the gospel or have I lost that confidence?" One is tempted to say, "Does this not go without saying? Is it not perfectly natural that a preacher or lay witness should hold this confidence?" We wish the issue could be dismissed that easily.

We are convinced that we continue to face a considerable crisis at this point. Our conversations with others have uncovered a lack of confidence in the act of witnessing and, more significantly, a lack of confidence that God will disclose God's self in the proclamation.

We should not be surprised at this. For several years preaching and testimony were downplayed in certain sections of the church. As someone remarked, "the pulpit was being robbed of its pull!" Critics of preaching were insisting that the sermon had little future and no worthy function in the emerging church, and testimony was dismissed as mere wallowing in subjective autobiography.

Therefore, not only were Christians discouraged from speaking, some were even forbidden to do so. Those who ventured to make their witness, despite this negativism and repression, were often held in contempt and caricatured by the very church that should have offered encouragement and support.

We were told that preaching was passe; that it was far too authoritarian in a time of "doing your own thing"; that you discovered truth by discussion. We were told that revelation never happens monologically but dialogically. We were told in preaching classes that our people are about as alert as chickens on a roost! We were told that if we have truth to convey then we ought not to spoil it by preaching it![16] As a result, according to Leander Keck, the modern witness became very much like "Lazarus in the pulpit" . . . his hands and feet bound with bandages and his face wrapped with a cloth . . . lifeless. Thus, the witness sometimes mounted the pulpit saying, "not even the best sermon will make a difference in this place!"[17]

With these attitudes, preaching and testimony become an exercise in futility. The speaker is aiming at nothing and hitting it hard! He or she is saying something as if it were nothing, or worse, saying nothing at all! If the pastor or lay speaker feels that his or her task is ludicrous, then, of course, they will fail. People in the pews lose confidence when they are not sure that the speaker really believes what he or she is saying. John Wesley once said, "It is of no little value that a preacher believes what he says." Strong witnessing is *confident* witnessing. It is believing that what you say is worth living and dying for.

Why the Loss of Confidence?

Why has there been a loss of confidence in testimony and preaching? Who or what is responsible? Is it the fault of the laity? The answer to this question seems to be a resounding *no*! The pastor's ability to preach remains a number one expectation as far as the laity are concerned. Dr. David H. C. Read, in his Lyman Beecher lectures, discovered that the lack of confidence in verbal witnessing cannot be laid at the door of the laity. He said, "It is worth noting . . . that the current disparagement of the sermon is almost exclusively a clerical phenomenon."[18] Why, then, does this persist? What accounts for it?

A number of factors account for this lack of confidence.[19] First, the context for preaching and testifying has radically changed. Neither the church context nor the cultural context now provides the support it once provided. We all know that historic Protestant Christianity exalted the spoken Word. This is still true wherever there is serious consideration given to the fundamental teachings of the Reformation. Karl Barth founded much of his theology on the belief that theology is an attempt to understand what happens when we testify and preach. Proof of this can be seen in the exalted and central position given to the pulpit in Protestant church architecture.

In Europe and in the United States, evangelical Christianity developed the Sunday evening service to strengthen the position of verbal witnessing. In the southern Appalachian mountains, as well as in other sections of our country, the Sunday evening service was once called the "evangelistic" service with emphasis on the spoken Word in preaching and testimony, while the Sunday morning service was called the "regular" worship service. In these same regions the pastor was seldom called by his proper or family name. He was often referred to as "preacher."

Still, the paramount place of testimony and preaching has been greatly reduced. There was a time when the thunder from a New York pulpit made saloon keepers and red light districts close down. History teaches us that governments in Great Britain could be brought down by the voice of the great nonconformist preachers. There was a time when the preacher was the "parson," that is "the person." This often meant that the preacher was one of the best educated persons in the community. Therefore, the pastor could rest assured that the Sunday sermon would be discussed not only over the Sunday meal but throughout the week wherever the people gathered. Today, however, the Sunday morning message proclaimed from the pulpit of a local church has numerous rivals both inside and outside the church.

There was a time when testimony was a key element in Christian worship. It was not unusual for Christians to offer a verbal witness. It was an expected and appreciated form of Christian stewardship. Testimony was considered to be a helpful and major means of confirming one's own faith and in bringing others to faith in Jesus Christ.

There was a time when small group meetings were given over to testimony. The early Methodist class meetings encouraged people to verbalize their relationship with God. Witnessing within the Christian community became a practice session which prepared the people of God to bear witness in their homes, at work, and in the marketplaces. Today, however, in many parts of the church, one rarely hears a testimony given as a part of the worship life of the congregation. And unfortunately, some small groups fail to encourage members to verbalize their faith and tell of their own Christian pilgrimage.

In some parts of the world, radio and television have brought preaching and testimony into the home. People can remain at home in the comfort of their living rooms and listen to or "watch" a worship service in much the same way as they watch a sporting event or listen to their favorite rock star or soap opera. All over the world, people can listen in on religious broadcasting via the transistor radio and audiotape. In addition, church programming has become so diversified that verbal witnessing tends to be squeezed out. Today, instead of having Sunday evening evangelistic services, some churches provide programs that vary all the way from basket weaving to yoga. At the same time, the regular Sunday morning worship has become increasingly elaborate. As a result, sermons grow shorter and shorter and there is no time for personal testimony.

Demands on the preacher's time make it increasingly difficult to adequately prepare. Because of expectations on the part of parishioners and denominational leaders, pastors must perform many duties. Unfortunately, when it seems that there are not enough hours in the day, that portion of the preacher's work which usually suffers most is his or her prayer and study time. If the preacher is to have adequate study and prayer time for reflection, he or she must guard that time with fierce jealousy. Otherwise, an avalanche of responsibilities will smother out the time necessary for adequate preparation. Bishop Arthur J. Moore used to say, "Jonah was swallowed by a whale. The modern preacher is being nibbled to death by minnows!" These realities caused Jack London to admonish preachers during their study time to put the following sign on their office door: "Do not enter without knocking," and beneath that he wrote: "Do not knock!"

What About the Laity?

Equally critical is the dilemma faced by lay leaders. Today's busy lifestyle tends to consume the average lay person. As someone said, "Lay people are so busy making a living that they fail to make a life." Caught up in a whirlwind of endless activity, the lay person experiences great difficulty in finding room for study, prayer, and reflection. We can fill our hands so full of papers, printouts, and reports that we cannot find room for a book, especially that book called the Bible. One must seriously prepare in order to witness effectively. Lack of preparation leads to shallow and ineffective testimony.

Cultural changes have also greatly eroded the support once enjoyed by testimony and preaching. Television has made it difficult to gain and sustain interest in a verbal presentation without accompanying drama. We may argue with Marshal McLuhan's contention that we have moved from the age of print and talk to the age of the visual—the electronic age—but it is quite clear that something rather dramatic has happened to our ability to perceive verbal communication.

What Has Happened?

1. Human sensibilities have been blunted by the impact of the media bombardment. We hear, see, and experience so much that we tend to become calloused to it all. Americans can choose from more than 25,000 items on supermarket shelves, tune in as many as 53 television stations, buy any of 11,092 magazines or periodicals, and be solicited by thousands of special interest groups selling their wares or protecting their turf. We are becoming over-whelmed, even paralyzed by and apathetic to all these choices and possibilities. This avalanche of increasing choices is leaving people stymied by trivial matters. Laboratory tests on humans and animals conducted in the 1950s and 1960s, demonstrated that reaction time slows as choices increase.[20]

This has created an age of distraction—an age in which little is absorbed from the media bombardment. The dangers are obvious. Triviality could supplant fundamental reality and reduce people to passivity when it comes to social ills, global events, even local elections. We become so calloused and apathetic that we are no longer embarrassed by sin. As the prophet Jeremiah put it, "We lose the ability to blush" (Jer. 6:15). We acquiesce to permissiveness, violence, and injustice. Traditionally, we have been taught that there are two basic forms of sin: sins of omission and sins of commission. However, there is a third form of sin, and it is far more insidious in terms of its impact upon human community: sins of permission. That is, we simply acquiesce to sin and evil and never lift a voice or a finger to stop it.

2. A second factor contributing to this inability to perceive verbal communication is the fact that people have developed a built-in suspicion of all communicators and all communication. Research has shown that the number of Americans who consider advertising believable has plunged from 47 percent to 35 percent since 1973. The number of Americans who consider celebrity endorsers as believable has dropped from 22 percent five years ago to only 16 percent today.[21] The slick politician bombards our minds with slogans "in 20 second T.V. bites," but we have learned to take them with a grain of salt. It has been reported that the average church member in America is exposed, in one week's time, to twenty minutes of preaching and nine hours of television commercials. However, many people are becoming aware of the highly manipulative and even subliminal techniques that underlie these commercials. For our own protection there is a tendency to develop a suspicion about the integrity of the communicator. Preachers and lay speakers are increasingly aware of this suspicion, and sometimes it causes us to succumb to a negative attitude toward our own attempts at communication. Thus we lose confidence.

We are becoming aware that, for the most part, television has very little to say. Sometimes it has absolutely nothing to say. However, it does say it as if it were something! On the other hand, preachers and lay speakers do have something important to say, but alas, we sometimes say it as if it were nothing! In our negativism, we react by going in the opposite direction. We do not wish to be identified with the empty-headedness often exemplified in television programming. However, in overreacting we become increasingly dull. Some clergy and laity stand in the pulpit as if their presence there was expected, though unnecessary. Paul Scherer says, "Then it is that body and blood slip out of all the transactions of that place, and there abides with the preacher's people nothing but the uneasy memory of an hour scarcely more authentic than the starched rhetoric which tries to fill it."[22]

Scherer goes on to describe an experience that Ralph Waldo Emerson had when he attended church on a snowy day and was sorely tempted never to go again. Emerson describes this experience as follows:

> The snow storm was real; the preacher merely spectral, and the eye felt the sad contrast in looking at him and then out of the window behind him, into the beautiful meteor of the snow. He had no word intimating that he had laughed or wept, was married or in love, had been commended, or cheated, or chagrined. If he had ever lived or acted, we were none the wiser for it. The capital secret of his profession, namely, to convert life into truth, he had not learned.[23]

With tongue-in-cheek, Fred Craddock says, "Let the salesperson be lively and brilliant with a bar of soap, but let the person who speaks to and for the church be neither lively nor brilliant."[24]

3. Another factor contributing to the loss of confidence has been that of the witnesses' credibility—or lack of it. It is hard to take witnessing seriously because it is hard to take the witness seriously! The advocate's credibility has been greatly impaired by a number of factors. The sex and hush money scandal that knocked some evangelists from atop the religious television empire provided many Americans with a real-life soap opera. People were given daily reminders of the financial practices of some television evangelists and the lack of accountability in some religious organizations. Given the cult of personality that surrounds some of these television evangelists and their celebrity endorsers and the millions of dollars involved in their operations, it was only a matter of time before some of them fell. With a sense of sadness, as well as a blend of outrage, amusement, and, no doubt, prurient

interest, the public learned of these failures. These machina-
tions, plus a rather thorough exposure of the opulent lifestyle
of some televangelists have tended to bring discredit to
testimony and preaching in the minds of many and have left
much misery and suspicion in their wake. For many years
evangelists (lay and clergy) have been saying to the world,
"repent and believe the gospel." Today, however, the world
is saying to the church "repent and practice the gospel." If
one listens one can almost hear echoes of the challenge to
Jesus: "Doctor, cure yourself" (Luke 4:23).

4. Christian preaching and testimony have been impaired
because preachers and lay witnesses have often mounted the
ramparts and faced the wrong way on critical issues such a
world peace, hunger, empowerment of oppressed groups,
racism, and sexism. Rather than possessing the prophets
scorn of tyranny, some preachers and lay witnesses have
tended to bow the knee to Baal. They have oriented their
message more to our secular, selfish culture than to the
kingdom of God. This has significantly eroded confidence in
testimony and preaching. The speaker's credibility is not only
based upon lifestyle (*ethos*); it is also based upon the content
of his or her message.

Some witnesses have failed to be faithful to the message of
the kingdom of God. In so doing, they have pandered to
people's selfish wants rather than addressing basic needs.
We do believe that people who respond positively to the
gospel receive salvation as a gracious gift, and with it the
assurance of eternal life. It is, however, not the primary
purpose of testimony and preaching to impart to people
such guaranteed happiness, neither for this world nor the
next. Christ gives people joy, hope, trust, vision, and
courage in this life, and a promise of blessedness for all
eternity. If the offer of the benefits gets center stage in our
testimony and preaching, that is, if the message becomes
the offer of a psychological panacea, then the gospel of the

kingdom is degraded to a consumer product and does indeed become the opiate of the people. This distorted form of preaching and testimony fosters a self-centeredness whose chief aim is personal fulfillment. This reduces preaching and testimony to a television commercial where the call to conversion is presented in a "things-go-better-with-Jesus"wrapping.

The theologian, Karl Barth, addresses this issue. He admits that some Christian teaching, preaching, and testimony have tended to regard Christians as enjoying an indescribably magnificent private good fortune. This highlights a person's personal experience of grace and salvation as the chief concern. Barth regards all of this as thoroughly unbiblical and egocentric. He argues that the personal enjoyment of salvation in no way becomes the central theme of the Bible. He is not saying that the enjoyment of salvation is wrong, unimportant, and unbiblical. Rather he is contending that these items are secondary. They are by-products. What makes a person a Christian is not only his or her personal experience of grace but his or her lifestyle and ministry.[25] These comments of Barth have tremendous consequences for our understanding of testimony and preaching. Gospel communication that stops at calling people to accept Christ is incomplete and truncated. The church exists for the world, not the world for the church, as if the world were a reservoir from which the church draws. It is not only to receive life that people are called to become Christians, but also to give life.

Therefore, kingdom-oriented preaching or testimony offers more than simply individual personal bliss. It calls people to become followers of Jesus, enlisting them for mission, a mission that is as comprehensive as that of Jesus. The credibility of gospel communication and the credibility of preachers and lay witnesses is compromised when we employ psychological and rhetorical devices to persuade people to accept Christ without any reference whatsoever to any positive attitude to, or involvement in, ministry in the world. This tends to imply that a person's personal and spiritual liberation has no implications on the social, economic, and political front. It leads to a form of "cheap grace" in which people are indeed challenged to accept Christ, and come to faith, but too often the challenge is issued in respect to those areas of life where conversion will not be too costly.

Preaching and testimony that take on these negative features usually produce a certain kind of church. Whenever the church's involvement in society becomes secondary and optional, whenever the church invites people to take refuge in the name of Jesus without challenging the principalities and powers, it becomes a countersign of the kingdom. When compassionate ministry is subordinated to the preaching of a message of individual salvation, the church is offering "cheap grace" to people. Consequently, the content of the gospel is a "conscience-soothing Jesus, an unscandalous cross, an otherworldly kingdom, a private, inwardly spirit, a pocket God, a spiritualized Bible, and an escapist church."[26] For the church, this results in a fortress mentality that implies once we get inside, then hell cannot reach us. This is a far cry from the image given by Jesus that features a church against which "the gates of Hades will not prevail" (Matt. 16:18).

Since the gospel is indeed the good news of the kingdom, and since the kingdom is the detailed expression of God's caring reign over the whole of life, and since the goal of testimony and preaching is that of initiating people into the kingdom of God, then we are to proclaim a message about God whose nature is to uphold justice, mercy, and equity, to watch over the circumstances of strangers, widows, and orphans, to help the sick, and to liberate the poor and the prisoners. Only as this message is fervently believed, practiced, and preached can credibility be established for the lay witness or preacher. Only when credibility is established can confidence be restored.

We believe that we are turning the corner on this issue. Increasingly, in our country, as well as in other parts of the world, there is a hunger to hear the Word of God proclaimed with confidence. There is a new wave of interest in preaching and testimony and this bodes well for the Christian movement world-wide. The widespread tendency to downgrade the importance of preaching and testimony is being reversed and this is producing not only a revival of interest in witnessing but a revival of Christianity itself. As Dr. Leander Keck says, "Every renewal of Christianity has been accompanied by a renewal of preaching."[27]

We are discovering that pastors and lay persons are experiencing renewed confidence in the spoken word. Some are discovering the kind of confidence exemplified in this statement made by pastor Johannes Hamel of what was formerly called East Germany:

> When we preach in the name of Jesus Christ, we are proclaiming a reality so immense that the very naming of it basically changes the situation of the hearer, because this is the event of all events. Where the Gospel is preached, demons are robbed of their power; sins are forgiven; prisoners are freed; and the sorrowing are made joyful: God's wrath is turned to loving kindness. This and nothing less than this occurs with the preaching of the Gospel.

This is confidence! It is confidence in God, in the Word of God, and confidence in the act of testimony and preaching. When this kind of scriptural confidence is present, the witness will proclaim the message incessantly whether the occasion is favorable or not, whether results are forthcoming or not. This kind of confidence, rooted in scripture and born of the Holy Spirit, empowers the redeemed of the Lord to say so!

Part Two

Content of Preaching and Testifying

Chapter Four

The Message of Jesus

We have considered the biblical mandate to "let the redeemed of the Lord say so." We have made a strong case for verbal witnessing, shown the importance of preaching and testifying, and highlighted the need for renewed confidence in this essential ministry of the church. We must now focus on the content of the message.

A witness in a secular law court gives testimony to events. A Christian witness testifies to the deeds and events of God. The one who testifies never begins with a blank page. There is a story to be told, a song to be sung, and an event to be proclaimed. Preaching and testifying are the primary means of telling the story of what God has done, is doing, and will do.

As stated earlier, in the law courts "witness" and "testimony" are words that refer to the body of evidence that provides proof. This is precisely what Paul means when he writes to the church at Corinth:

> I must remind you of the gospel that I preached to you; the gospel which you received, on which you have taken your stand, and which is now bringing you salvation. Do you still hold fast the gospel as I preached it to you? If not, your conversion was in vain. First and foremost, I handed on to you the facts which had been imparted to me: that Christ died for our sins, in accordance with the scriptures; that he was buried;

that he was raised to life on the third day, according to the
scriptures; and that he appeared to Cephas, and afterwards to
the Twelve. Then he appeared to over five hundred of our
brothers at once, most of whom are still alive, though some
have died. Then he appeared to James, and afterwards to all
the apostles (1 Cor. 15:1-7, NEB).

There is a body of evidence, a gospel on which we take our
stand. "Taking the stand" is imagery used to describe the act
of testifying. We often refer to one who gives evidence in a
court of law as "taking the stand."

When we take the stand, we do so with a message.
Therefore, witnessing is more than our autobiography, even
though our own personal experience is always involved. The
focus of our testimony is beyond ourselves and points toward
the biography of God's action. We do not make up a story.
This would mean that we are false witnesses. Clearly the focus
of the preaching and testifying of the early apostles is the
"word of the Lord," the good news of the kingdom of God
(Acts 8:25).

The content of the message of the gospel is critical if we are
to know the truth and to know the truth is critical if we are to
experience freedom (John 8:31-32). A lie always enslaves and
results in bondage. Thus, it behooves the witness to speak the
truth, the whole truth, and nothing but the truth!

In Christian witnessing we point away from ourselves and
toward Jesus, the Christ. Like the woman at the well (John 4),
we testify "Come and see a man" (John 4:29). Dr. Emilio
Castro, General Secretary of World Council of Churches,
states "In a jungle of competitive offerings of miracle solutions
to all human problems, a finger pointing clearly to Jesus, the
Lamb of God is the best service we can render to the world
today."[1] We can do no greater service in our preaching and
testifying than pointing a finger to Jesus.

If we are to take seriously the task of witnessing, we must know the facts as they have been handed on to us from the message of Jesus, the early church, and the Wesleyan tradition.

It is critical for those of us who preach, teach, and testify to know the central message of Jesus. If we are trying to reach a new destination and we do not know the way, what do we need? A map? Yes, but what if there are no clearly marked roads? In response to this question, a man in India said, "You had better find someone who has been there before and follow him." Indeed, this is a good and wise word. We are called to follow the One who has traveled this road before us. We must look "to Jesus the pioneer and perfecter of our faith" (Heb. 12:2).

According to Mark, Jesus came into Galilee proclaiming the kingdom of God. The summary of Jesus' message can be found in Mark 1:15: "The time is fulfilled and the kingdom of God is at hand; repent, and believe in the Gospel" (NAS). Scholars agree that the kingdom theme is the core of the preaching and teaching of Jesus.[2]

In the prophetic literature of the Old Testament and in the Psalms, the kingdom theme represents God's active and sovereign rule over all creation (Ps. 145:10-13). This is why we must offer the gospel to the whole world and all creation (Mark 16:15). This kingdom theme was celebrated in the Jewish temple, taught in the homes and later proclaimed in the synagogues. The whole history of Israel was to be a continuous affirmation of God's sovereignty over the world and the accountability of every living thing to its sovereign Lord. Moreover, in the Old Testament (as well as in the New Testament) there is the idea of God's kingdom as a future hope, that is, the promise of a new world order. This new world order features a condition of peace and justice between peoples, nations, sexes, generations, races, and all human-kind and nature (Isa. 11:6ff; 11–12; 19:18; 42:4; and 51:4;

Jer. 31–33; and Amos 5:24). The kingdom of God anticipates the transformation of the entire created order. There is to be a new heaven and a new earth (Isa. 65:17; Rev. 21:22).

The preaching of Jesus presupposed the sovereign rule of God. Therefore, the hope of the kingdom that was expressed by the prophets became the focus of his teaching. The good news he came preaching was the announcement of the messianic age, a whole new world order. He believed that God was in the process of inaugurating the kingdom. He went beyond the prophets, however, in announcing the breakthrough of this new world order. He believed that in him the new world order had come within the reach of every human being. Is it any wonder that the phrases "kingdom of God" and "kingdom of heaven" are used by Jesus one hundred twenty-two times in the synoptic Gospels of Matthew, Mark, and Luke? The reign of God is the primary message of Jesus.

The Compass for Preaching and Testifying

The central place of the kingdom of God can be illustrated by a compass. A compass points the direction for pilgrims who are traveling a new way. It enables pilgrims to reach the intended destination even in strange and unfamiliar surroundings. The center of the compass is the reign/kingdom of God, and every critical reference point on the compass is seen through the center of the compass.

Creation

For instance, in creation the reign of God is expressed in terms of visible reality. God spoke and creation happened. God declares creation good and male and female very good. Moreover, in creation everything fitted together in perfect harmony. There was no hint of slavery or bondage in creation. One part of creation did not dominate or destroy the other. As we are often reminded, before there was original sin there was original righteousness.

Humans are intended to be stewards of creation, caring for the land, the sea, and the sky and all living creatures. Created in the image of God, humans are given the freedom to love or to abuse and destroy creation. Thus, an important point on the compass is creation, for in creation we see the reign of God established.

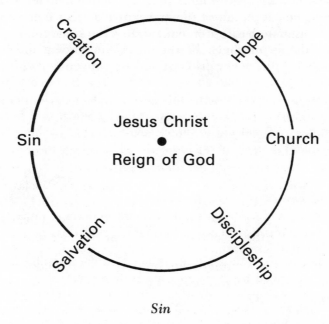

Sin

Humanity chooses to turn away from the reign of God and the perfect harmony of creation. The result is alienation and bondage. An important point on the compass has to do with the nature of sin. In their attempt to make self the center of the universe, human beings yield to the ultimate temptation of trying to have it all and attempt to supplant the authority of God. Sin manifests itself not only within human beings and human relations, it also expresses itself in social, economic, and political structures.

Three current movements in the world express the ultimate lie and give evidence of the consequence of rebellion against the rule of God. In South Africa, Apartheid is an institutionalized system built on a lie. The system's premise rests upon the lie that one person is superior to another person because of the color of the skin. An entire system of determining a person's existence, education, home, vocation, identity, and worth is constructed on a foundation with a lie at its center. A system that is built upon a lie always enslaves all the people who are under that system. Both the oppressed and the oppressor end up in bondage.

Another movement in the world that enslaves people is that found in Eastern Europe. During the first half of the twentieth century a political system emerged in Eastern Europe that had at its core an atheistic philosophy. Any system that has at its center the ultimate lie, "There is no God," will eventually enslave people. President Vaclav Havel of Czechoslovakia, speaking to the Congress of the United States of America on February 21, 1990, less than three months after the "bloodless revolution" of his country, said:

> When they arrested me on October 27, 1989, I was living in a country ruled by the most conservative communist government in Europe and our society slumbered beneath the pall of a totalitarian system. When a people or system abdicates its responsibility to truth, it results in slavery and bondage. Slavery is a waste of the creation of God.

Capitalistic consumerism (a belief or policy that says one can have it all) is another rampant, greedy movement in the world that ends up enslaving people. Like a tiny hamster in its small cage with its little wheel, many persons in Western societies end up trapped in their cages and going round and round the merry-go-round of life. Believing the lie that these new goods, possessions, or fame will bring meaning or fulfillment, many become addicted and enslaved to the power of fortune and/or fame. In many affluent societies there are millions of people so seriously addicted to alcohol, sex, gambling, or other addictions that they have no sense or capacity for decisions in their lives. Living the lie always enslaves.

These three illustrations express the truth of Paul's message, "For the wages of sin is death" (Rom. 6:23*a*). Here we understand the radical nature of human bondage and slavery and how human sin affects the whole of creation. Evil destroys and sin enslaves (Rom. 6:6). Yielding to the ultimate lie results in bondage unto death.

Salvation

The next point on the compass focuses on the deeds of God that make salvation possible. The message to which we give witness is that God does not turn away from creation. God pursues humanity through the prophets and the chosen community. God calls Israel to be a light unto all nations and to take the message of God's salvation to all people, even those in Nineveh. (See the book of Jonah.)

The ultimate, full, complete revelation of God's kingdom comes in one born to a peasant girl, a virgin named Mary in an obscure village called Bethlehem. Here we have an amazing paradox. At a time when there was an impersonal census being taken under the order of a Roman emperor who commanded everyone to be counted like sheep, God acted in a personal way so that everyone would be given a proper name!

The ministry of Jesus is one of saving people and calling them by name: Simon, Andrew, Mary, Zacchaeus. His ministry is to set people free to enter and live in terms of the kingdom of God. To a religious official named Nicodemus, Jesus speaks of the possibility of being born again. This new birth results in a person's being able to see and to enter the kingdom of God (John 3:5).

It is necessary to discern the signs of the kingdom. A part of redemption is recognition, being able to see and noticing that which has always been there from the beginning.[3] For Jesus, salvation is understood as seeing and entering the reign of God. He came to make it possible for us to be born again, to see the reign of God and to be initiated into that reign.

Discipleship

Discipleship, the fourth point on the compass, means living in terms of God's kingdom. We are saved—we see and enter the kingdom—but there is also a sense in which we are forever being saved (1 Cor. 15:2). Therefore, being saved involves a process of obedience to God's rule. It is no accident that the words *disciple* and *discipline* are so closely intertwined. When the disciples of John asked Jesus for evidence of his messiahship, he enumerated the following:

> The blind receive their sight, the lame walk, the lepers are cleansed, the deaf hear, the dead are raised, and the poor have good news brought to them. (Matt. 11:5)

In a similar fashion Jesus, in his inaugural address in Nazareth, lists the following marks of his kingdom ministry:

> The Spirit of the Lord is upon me,
> because he has anointed me
> to bring good news to the poor.
> He has sent me to proclaim release
> to the captives and recovery of sight to the
> blind, to let the oppressed go free, to
> proclaim the year of the
> Lord's favor. (Luke 4:18-19)

Jesus makes it clear that faithful discipleship involves performing these acts of ministry.

According to Matthew, the doing of these deeds provides the criteria for the final judgment of the nations and people when they come before the Lord. The questions are clear and direct: Have we fed the hungry and given drink to the thirsty? Have we welcomed the stranger? Have we visited those who are sick and those who are in prison? Have we given clothing to those who need it? Have we offered hope and good news to the lonely and desperate (Matt. 25:31-46)? Loving God and the neighbor are at the heart of discipleship. Trusting and obeying God is the kingdom lifestyle. It is like the chorus of the gospel song: "Trust and obey for there's no other way to be happy in Jesus, but to trust and obey."[4] To be a disciple of Jesus is to live as Jesus lived, to do the deeds of the kingdom of God.

The Church

According to the scripture, the church is a primary expression of the reign of God. The church in its concrete reality is a part of the gospel. It is a part of the action of God for the salvation of the world. Therefore, the church is a crucial point on the compass. When it is authentic, the church is an awesome community. This is clearly expressed in the early church immediately following Pentecost. Awe gripped the early followers of Christ as they devoted themselves to the teachings of the apostles, prayer, fellowship, and breaking of bread. "Awe came upon everyone, because many wonders and signs were being done by the apostles" (Acts 2:43). The people were overwhelmed with incredible joy as they praised God and enjoyed the good will of all the people.

Though the church is not synonymous with the kingdom, it is the primary instrument of God's mission in the world. It is called to the task of making visible the signs of the kingdom. Jesus called a group of ordinary people, taught them the message of the kingdom, and initiated them into it. He called forth a community of persons who would not only live in the present reality of the kingdom, but would also live in hope of the fulfillment of the kingdom.

Hope

The final point on our compass for preaching and testifying is hope. The church lives in hope. When we preach or testify, we speak of the kingdom that has come, is come, and will come. We proclaim the dawn of this new age in Jesus Christ, and testify to a kingdom that will be fully consummated. Thus, we are a people who live in hope, and it is this expectant hope which sustains us as we live in the meantime. No matter how difficult the circumstances of the present, we know God's reign will be victorious.

There is a future realization of the kingdom. Norman Perrin affirms how Jesus looked toward the day when that which was inaugurated in his own ministry would be fulfilled. This truth can be seen in the parables. The parables of Jesus are parables of hope. Like a tiny mustard seed, the kingdom is now present, but one day it will become a bush in which the birds make their nest. Like yeast in the dough, today it is small, tomorrow it fills the whole container. So it is with the kingdom. One can be sure of the kingdom's present reality, and one can look with expectant hope toward its ultimate fulfillment.

It is this expectant hope that raises Christian witnesses to tiptoe and motivates us to speak the truth. Looking toward the future fulfillment of the kingdom does not take away from the present, it gives meaning to the present. Carl E. Braaten in an unpublished manuscript says, "Modern medical psychology has confirmed this insight: Hope is an essential factor in the recovery of health; the absence of hope accelerates the hour of death." This teaches us that hopelessness is a form of death to those still living.

But hope is evoked in the Christian as a result of the good news of the kingdom. The hope of the kingdom enables persons to live in the tension between the present and the future. Perrin encourages us to:

> hold fast to the conviction that the consummation of that which was begun in the ministry of Jesus *will be* and that it will be just as much a reality to be experienced as was the beginning in the ministry of Jesus and in the experience of those who first believed in him. How? when? where? may be natural questions but they are illegitimate questions in view of the fact that the teaching of Jesus seems deliberately to avoid anything that could be construed as an answer to them (Mark 13:32). This teaching puts the emphasis where it belongs: In the state of tension between present and future in which the believer must live and move and have his being.[5]

This eschatological pull of the dynamic kingdom of God is a major incentive in preaching and testifying. It energizes the church. One of the most consistent and persistent tasks of our day is to kindle the true hope of the gospel of the kingdom. For the citizen of the kingdom of God, it is not a bad thing to look down the corridor of time and see that the door is open to the future. God has opened the door from the other side. Jesus tears down the No Exit sign from the door of tomorrow. Thus, the future is filled with promise and hope. Christians pray with confident hope, "Thy kingdom come, thy will be done on earth as it is in heaven."

Sign of the Kingdom

When Jesus came into Galilee proclaiming, "The time is fulfilled and the kingdom of God has come near" (Mark 1:15), there were those who found it difficult to hear and accept his word. They asked Jesus for a sign of the kingdom (Matt. 12:38). He responded, "The only sign that will be given is the sign of the prophet Jonah" (Matt. 12:39). They remembered the prophet Jonah, and likewise we would do well to remember the prophet Jonah.

As previously noted, it was God who chose that the people of Nineveh should hear God's message. Jonah reluctantly preached the word of the Lord, and Nineveh repented. Nineveh did not ask for a sign, nor for a special demonstration of any kind. *The preaching of the prophet was a sufficient sign!*

In recalling this story, Jesus insists the same truth applies to every generation and place. The *necessary* sign of the kingdom is kingdom preaching and testifying. Jesus himself came preaching and testifying. He issued the invitation, "Repent and believe this good news of the reign of God." Like Jonah we are often reluctant to preach and testify, but God wants the "Ninevehs" all over the world to be saved. God desires that none should be lost.

Like Jonah, we often endeavor to escape our calling to preach and testify, but God pursues us. Jonah was in the whale's belly for three days and nights. But Jonah came forth from the belly of the whale and preached as one who had come back from a darkened pit. D. T. Niles observes that God's love had captured Jonah, a love so great that it would let neither him nor Nineveh go.[6]

Using the experience of Jonah, Jesus refers to his own death and burial. Jesus says, "For three days and three nights the Son of Man will be in the heart of the earth" (Matt. 12:40). He applauds Nineveh for repenting simply because of the witness of Jonah. He affirms that a greater one than Jonah is now present. In anticipation of Jesus' resurrection, he makes it clear that the bonds of death shall be broken, the victorious Christ revealed, and his kingdom will know no end. The only appropriate response to the risen Christ is to repent and believe the good news.

Pastors and lay persons have the responsibility to hold forth the centrality of the ministry of Jesus and the message of the kingdom of God. We hear our Lord saying, "Seek first the kingdom of God" (Matt. 6:33 KJV).

As kingdom people we are committed to seeing, proclaiming, and doing the signs of the kingdom. Our message is the message of Jesus. With the message of Jesus burning in our hearts, we can do no other than speak out. *Let the redeemed of the Lord say so!*

Chapter Five

The Message Goes Forth

T he early church "testified and spoke the word of the Lord" (Acts 8:25). After the resurrection, Jesus remained with the disciples for forty days, giving evidence that he was alive and "speaking about the kingdom of God" (Acts 1:3). He prepared his disciples for his departure by assuring them of the coming of the Holy Spirit to give them power to be his "witnesses in Jerusalem, in all Judea and Samaria, and to the ends of the earth" (Acts 1:8). The Spirit came on the day of Pentecost, and the result was the preaching and testifying that Jesus is the Christ.

The message proclaimed by Peter on the day of Pentecost gives evidence of the early church's conviction regarding Jesus, the Messiah.

> You that are Israelites, listen to what I have to say: Jesus of Nazareth, a man attested to you by God with deeds of power, wonders, and signs that God did through him among you, as you yourselves know—this man . . . you crucified. . . . But God raised him up, having freed him from death, because it was impossible for him to be held in its power. (Acts 2:22-24)

Peter continued giving evidence that God has acted to make Jesus Lord, the anointed one of God: "This Jesus God raised up, and of that all of us are witnesses" (Acts 2:32).

The people who heard in their own language responded to the message by being convicted in their hearts and cried out, "Brothers, what should we do?" (Acts 2:37) Without any hesitation Peter called for them to "Repent and be baptized every one of you in the name of Jesus Christ" (Acts 2:38).

The Christian church took root and grew when Peter stood up and witnessed. When we are tempted to lose confidence in preaching and testifying, we need to remember what Paul said: "God decided, through the foolishness of our proclamation, to save those who believe" (1 Cor. 1:21). Preaching and testimony are still involved in the birthing of churches. We must never forget that proclamation was one of the first Pentecostal gifts. From this we learn there is no substitute for the ministry of impassioned speech. As long as there is an authentic church, there will be preaching and testimony. How else shall we confront this world except as we stand up like Peter of long ago and proclaim the mighty deeds of God?

The central place of Jesus Christ in the preaching and testifying of the apostles can be seen in the very first act of ministry after the day of Pentecost. When Peter and John were on their way to the Temple to pray, they encountered a man who had been lame from his birth. The man was asking for alms. Peter and John looked directly and steadfastly at the man, reminiscent of the manner in which Jesus looked intently at the people who reached out to him. They declared that they had no silver or gold but they would give him what they had. Peter said, "In the name of Jesus Christ of Nazareth, stand up and walk" (Acts 3:6). Later, when Peter and John stood at the portico of the Temple, they responded to the astonishment of the people regarding the healing of the lame man by making it clear that it was through faith in the *name of Jesus* that the man was made whole (Acts 3:16).

Even when confronted by the religious authorities and called upon to defend their actions, Peter and John held to the central message of Jesus Christ as the sovereign one whom God has exalted. Jesus of Nazareth is the foundation of their faith and the source of their boldness. They said:

> This Jesus is
>> "the stone that was rejected by
>> you, the builders;
>> it has become the
>> cornerstone."
>
> There is salvation in no one else, for there is no other name under heaven given among mortals by which we must be saved. (Acts 4:11-12)

This Jesus about whom the apostles preached and testified was the center of the message (Acts 4:18, 20). The early church spoke powerfully of what God had done. "With great power the apostles gave their testimony to the resurrection of the Lord Jesus, and great grace was upon them all" (Acts 4:33). Continually, the apostles spoke of how God "raised up Jesus" (Acts 5:30). Without ceasing they taught and proclaimed Jesus as the Messiah (Acts 5:42).

After his conversion Paul began to proclaim Jesus as the Son of God and the Messiah (Acts 9:20-22). The church pushed beyond Israel in its witness to the Gentile world, and it continued the message: "Jesus Christ—he is Lord of all" (Acts 10:36). "We are witnesses to all that he did" (Acts 10:39). Clearly these early followers understood their commission and mandate:

> He commanded us to preach to the people and to testify that he is the one ordained by God as judge of the living and of the dead. All the prophets testify about him that everyone who believes in him receives forgiveness of sins through his name. (Acts 10:42-43)

In his book, *Evangelism in the Early Church*, Michael
Green summarizes the message of the early church. First,
"they proclaimed a person," and the person was Jesus of
Nazareth. Second, "they offered a gift." It was the gift of
forgiveness, new life in the Spirit, and reconciliation. Third,
"they looked for a response." Without apology the disciples
called for the response of repentance, faith, obedience, and
baptism.[7]

The early church believed and preached that in Jesus the
kingdom of God had dawned. Jesus Christ established a new
world order:

> So if anyone is in Christ, there is a new creation: everything old
> has passed away; see, everything has become new! All this
> is from God, who reconciled us to himself through Christ.
> (2 Cor. 5:17-18*a*)

The early church was convinced that a new sovereign had
been revealed. They knew that it was impossible to have a
kingdom without a king. The reality of the kingdom could not
be divorced from its sovereign Lord. The church believed
that the kingdom of God as taught by Jesus was indeed
inaugurated by him.

We must not attempt to separate the message of Jesus from
the message of the apostles. There is no division in the
message of salvation in Jesus Christ and the message of the
kingdom of God. All New Testament witnessing is kingdom
oriented. The claim on the part of some that there is a hiatus
in the Bible between the mission to the Jews and the mission
to the rest of the world, or the claim that once Jesus Christ
became the content of the good news the kingdom was no
longer preached, simply will not stand up under New
Testament exegesis. The reign of God is central in the
proclamation of Jesus as well as the preaching and testifying of
the apostles. Always the early church spoke of God raising up
Jesus and anointing him. For Paul, God acted decisively in

Jesus Christ in order to realign or establish just relationships between humanity and God, among human beings, and with the whole ecological environment. The content of Paul's preaching was the justice and righteousness of God and he meant by that an event, a happening, or something coming into history and transforming it.[8] This is precisely what Jesus meant by the kingdom of God.

When the first apostles began to preach the good news of Jesus Christ (Acts 5:42, 8:35, 11:20), that certainly did not mean they ceased to announce the kingdom of God. The message of the kingdom of God included the whole of the preaching of Jesus and his apostles.[9]

Luke tells us that the disciples announced the "good news about the kingdom of God and the name of Jesus Christ" (Acts 8:12). They understood, as we must, that Jesus and the kingdom are intimately connected. On several occasions we read of Paul proclaiming the kingdom. During his final, very emotional meeting with the elders of the church at Ephesus, he reminded them that the proclamation of the kingdom was a central emphasis of his message (Acts 19:8, 20:25). It is interesting to note that as Luke closes his account of the Acts of the Apostles, he tells how Paul from daylight to dark testifies "to the kingdom of God" (Acts 28:23). In fact, the very last words of the two volumes written by Luke the physician, are:

> He [Paul] lived there [Rome] two whole years at his own expense
> and welcomed all who came to him, proclaiming the king-
> dom of God and teaching about the Lord Jesus Christ with
> all boldness and without hindrance. (Acts 28:30-31)

This is an intriguing scene. Paul, under house arrest, spends his last days bearing witness to the kingdom and giving testimony of Jesus the Christ. Thus, the book of Acts ends as it begins—focusing on the proclamation of the kingdom of God. This is precisely why the lordship of Jesus

Christ is such a central issue in New Testament witnessing. And it is also the reason why it is both unfaithful and absurd to call people to faith in Jesus Christ and not call people to the life of discipleship and obedience.

The church very early affirmed this key relationship of obedience to the will of God and the lordship of Jesus Christ. Paul challenged the believers to:

> Let the same mind be in you thàt was in Christ Jesus,
>   who, though he was in the form of God,
>   did not regard equality with God
>   as something to be exploited,
>   but emptied himself,
>   taking the form of a slave,
>   being born in human likeness.
>
> And being found in human form,
>   he humbled himself
>   and became obedient to the point of death—
>   even death on a cross.
>
> Therefore God also highly exalted him
>   and gave him the name
>   that is above every name,
> so that at the name of Jesus
>   every knee should bend,
>   in heaven and on earth and under the earth,
> and every tongue should confess
>   that Jesus Christ is Lord,
>   to the glory of God the Father.
>   (Philippians 2:5-11)

The first affirmation of faith in the early church was: "Jesus is Lord" (Rom. 10:9).

Even after Constantine, the church in its preaching and testifying did not abandon this central theme.[10] At the very

first ecumenical council of the church held at Nicea in
A.D. 329 the discussion focused on the person of Jesus. The
church attempted to put in words the central affirmation of
the church regarding Jesus the Christ. "We believe . . . in
one Lord, Jesus Christ, the only son of God . . . of one being
with the father for us and for our salvation he came down from
heaven . . ." (Nicene Creed). The church continued to
center its affirmations in Jesus. It preached and testified to
the mighty deeds of God in the life, death, and resurrection
of Jesus.

The church across the centuries has continued to preach
and testify to the deeds of God. We are recipients of this
message, and we are enriched by it. The message of St.
Francis, Augustine, Luther and many witnesses continue to
shape our story of faith.

The Message of Wesley

We are not followers of John Wesley. We are followers of
Jesus. We do, however, follow Jesus in the company of the
Wesleys—John, Charles, and Susanna. Therefore, it is
important to note the message of the Wesleys.

The late Albert Outler, premier scholar of Wesleyan
studies, points to the consistent theme of John Wesley's
preaching and testifying:

> The heart of Wesley's gospel was always its lively sense of
> God's grace at work at every level of creation and history in
> persons and communities.[11]

Such a vision of the gospel is strikingly related to Jesus'
central message on the reign of God, as well as the commission of our Lord to "Go into all the world and proclaim the
good news to the whole creation" (Mark 16:15).

It is no coincidence that Wesley records having preached
one hundred ninety times (more than on any other passage)

the text of Mark 1:15: "The time is fulfilled, and the kingdom of God has come near; repent, and believe in the good news." His sermon titled "The Way to the Kingdom" expresses Wesley's understanding of the kingdom of God. For him the kingdom of God is *true religion*. The first mark of *true religion* is loving God with all of one's heart, mind, soul, and strength. This is understood as righteousness.

The second mark of the kingdom is love of neighbor. For Wesley the neighbor is not only kinsfolk or those living nearby but every human being in need. Love for God and neighbor expresses itself in reconciliation, righteousness, and justice. True religion (hearts right with God and humanity) implies holiness, happiness, peace, and joy in the Holy Spirit.[12] Wesley believed the kingdom of God is the fruit of God's reign in the heart, soul, and all creation. This gift of grace brings new life. Wesley said, "God has given us eternal life. . . . 'He that hath the Son (reigning in his heart) hath life.'"[13] The aim of Wesley's preaching and testifying is repentance on the part of the hearers.

Because of the itinerate nature of his ministry and the mobility of the people, Wesley felt that each message must contain the essentials of the gospel. For him and for the people who heard him gladly, Wesley's message was the gospel of universal grace.[14] During the first year of the Methodist revival, after Aldersgate, he preached on 1 Cor. 1:30 more than seventy times:

> By God's act you are in Christ Jesus; God has made him our wisdom, and in him we have our righteousness, our holiness, our liberation. (REB)

Wesley continually emphasized "sufficient grace in all, irresistible grace in none."[15] He explicitly affirms universal grace without implying universal salvation and denying human freedom. Obviously there is a difference in universal grace and universal salvation.

Wesley was convinced that God had given a special calling of extraordinary ministry to the lay people. The responsibility for preaching and testifying belonged to the whole church. The Methodist revival was barely launched until Wesley began utilizing lay people to spread the gospel. Wesley, with reluctance, concluded that it was a fatal mistake to leave the task of spreading the gospel to the ordained clergy. There were too few clergy in the church to carry out this task, and there were too many clergy who were too stiff in their spiritual joints to get the job done. Intuitively, Wesley knew that battles are not fought by generals. In order to accomplish the task of taking the gospel to the whole world and all creation, Wesley knew he needed the spontaneity of those newly awakened souls coming forth from the revival. In order to fuel the revival, it was necessary to employ that contagion of spirit, that unstoppable witness of Christians recently set afire by the Holy Spirit. This decision, inspired by the Holy Spirit, made possible the tremendous expansion of the Wesleyan movement.

Wesley was a student of the New Testament. It was obvious to him that the evangelization of the early church was characterized by the fact that everyone was doing it. If one looks at the motley crowd which proclaimed the kingdom after Pentecost, one discovers that there was not a "real" clergy among them. They were lay persons, merely amateurs.

The contemporary Wesleyan movement has come through a period of high skepticism regarding the ministry of the laity. This skepticism can be witnessed in the credentialing processes for those persons who wish to follow full-time church-related vocations. We have been skeptical about the business of employing amateurs and trusting laypersons to do the sacred work of the Lord. We have felt that only those who were tested, trained, and credentialed could be trusted with the task of ministry. But the time has come for our movement to correct this narrowness and get back to the reality of Pentecost! We have been attempting to do the work of the kingdom with tried, tested, and properly credentialed saints, and we have not done it very well. Perhaps the time has come to emulate Jesus. Jesus chose the publicans and sinners to proclaim the kingdom. To read the New Testament is to be confronted with the wisdom of Jesus. He took these amateurs, these publicans and sinners, and gave them a task.

We would ask this question: Is there any reason why people should not be evangelists in their vocations? One of the most hopeful signs of renewal is the reemergence of the lay apostolate, the reemergence of the lay evangelist. One might call this the return of the amateur. The old notion that Christianity is the monopoly of ordained preachers and priests is being reappraised. The old idea, the preacher gets paid for being good and the layperson is good for nothing, is being discarded. There is a worldwide reawakening of the role of the layperson in the Christian movement.

We are beginning to see that the real heresy was in turning Christianity into a clergy dominated religion! This was never the intention of God. Christianity began as a lay movement. Jesus Christ was a carpenter. He was never a religious cleric, as we understand that term today. All of Jesus' disciples were laypersons, and the people on whom the Spirit descended at Pentecost were all laypersons. After the martyrdom of Stephen, a great persecution fell upon the Church of Jerusalem. The church was scattered throughout the region. The laypersons who were scattered went everywhere proclaiming the gospel (Acts 8:1-4). It was lay evangelism that carried the Good News in the first century.

In the final decade of the twentieth century, we must make more room for this development. We must deliberately evolve creative approaches to lay ministry. We must develop fresh and creative channels through which this divine energy can flow. As we have traveled around the world we have noticed that some of the most hopeful work in evangelism is being done by lay evangelists. Many laypersons are tired of being spectators. They want to do something more exciting than simply helping to fund the budget. Despite the fact that many lack a sophisticated theological approach and do not carry with them the prestige of the ordained minister, many are venturing into the arena and testifying their faith to their colleagues, as well as to the stranger in the street. In their very freshness and spontaneity, laypersons are infusing a new and creative spirit into the life of the church.

The time has come for the Wesleyan movement to broaden its understanding of ministry and make room for the amateur. The time has come for us to take seriously the model for evangelism developed in the first-century church and utilize what John Wesley rediscovered. We need to learn to trust the amateur, and the amateur needs to be trained and equipped for the work of ministry.

John Wesley felt that the gospel message must remain clear. As doctrinal pluralism developed in the Methodist movement, he gathered the preachers, primarily laypersons, who were being sent forth to preach and testify, and he prepared them for their ministry. In fulfilling this task, Wesley continually emphasized the essentials of the gospel. The following is a summary of these essentials:

1. God's grace is for all.
2. The bondage of sin is universal.
3. Salvation, redemption, and reconciliation are possible only through Jesus Christ.
4. The human response is repentance and trust.
5. The Holy Spirit grants assurance to the heart of those who trust in God through Jesus Christ.
6. Holiness of heart and life is the work of the Holy Spirit in the life of the church and the world.[16]

The essentials of the Wesleyan message were highlighted in the singing of the early Methodists. A brilliant summary of the essentials is found in Charles Wesley's hymn "Love Divine":

> Love divine, all loves excelling,
> Joy of heaven, to earth come down;
> Fix in us thy humble dwelling,
> All thy faithful mercies crown!
> Jesus, thou art all compassion,
> Pure, unbounded love thou art;
> Visit us with thy salvation;
> Enter every trembling heart.
>
> Breathe, O breathe thy loving spirit
> Into every troubled breast!
> Let us all in thee inherit;
> Let us find that second rest.
> Take away our bent to sinning;
> Alpha and Omega be;
> End of faith, as its beginning,
> Set our hearts at liberty.
>
> Come, Almighty to deliver,
> Let us all thy life receive;
> Suddenly return and never,
> Nevermore thy temples leave.
> Thee we would be always blessing,
> Serve thee as thy hosts above,
> Pray and praise thee without ceasing,
> Glory in thy perfect love.
>
> Finish, then, thy new creation;
> Pure and spotless let us be.
> Let us see thy great salvation
> Perfectly restored in thee:

> Changed from glory into glory,
> Till in heaven we take our place,
> Till we cast our crowns before thee,
> Lost in wonder, love, and praise.

The words of this hymn speak of the restoration of creation by the grace of divine love. As Wesley lay on his deathbed he struggled to express himself, asking, "Where is my sermon on the Love of God? Take it and spread it abroad."[17] His last reference to witnessing centered on the love and grace of God. Again and again in summarizing his message, Wesley declared: "We love because he first loved us" (1 John 4:19).

The content of our witnessing is simply and magnificently the old, old story of Jesus and his love. The heart of our preaching and testifying is the death and the resurrection of Jesus Christ (Luke 24:46). Like Paul, we preach and testify of the cross and the empty tomb (1 Cor. 2:2). Having experienced the cleansing power of the blood of Christ Jesus, we become Easter people and hallelujah is our song. With Paul we affirm:

> If Christ was not raised, then our gospel is null and void, and so too is your faith. And we turn out to have given *false* evidence (italics added) about God. . . . But the truth is Christ was raised to life. . . . For he is destined to reign. (1 Cor. 15:14-15, 20, 24, REB)

Our Christian experience enables us to testify firsthand. We have died with Christ, and we have risen with Christ. We are a part of a new kingdom with a new king and a new hope. Therefore, we take the stand declaring:

> Blessed be the God and Father of our Lord Jesus Christ! By his great mercy he has given us a new birth into a living hope through the resurrection of Jesus Christ from the dead, and into an inheritance that is imperishable, undefiled, and unfading. (1 Peter 1:3-4*a*)

As ambassadors of Christ we go forth, saying:

> All this is from God, who reconciled us to himself through
> Christ, and has given us the ministry of reconciliation; that is,
> in Christ God was reconciling the world to himself, not
> counting their trespasses against them, and entrusting the
> message of reconciliation to us. So we are ambassadors for
> Christ. . . . (2 Cor. 5:18-20a)

Recently on a visit to Shanghai, China, we visited a great
congregation known today as *Muen Church*, which literally
means taking a bath in Grace Church. This congregation was
closed by the Communists in 1969 along with congregations
throughout China. It was a time of great suffering and
oppression for Christians. Pastors and laity were exiled and
sentenced to hard labor. Christians were severely punished
for practicing their faith. During our visit with the pastors of
the church, we were deeply moved by their faith and
integrity. We asked, "When you were exiled from the city,
did you ever dream of worshiping in this sanctuary again?"
"No," each responded. "We thought maybe our children
would, but none of us ever imagined that we would pray or
sing again in this sanctuary."

During those ten years when the church building was
closed under the oppressive regime of the *gang of four*, the
building was turned into a government school. After the
death of the *gang of four* the building was reopened as a
church in 1979. As we walked into this magnificent church,
one of the pastors invited us to move toward the front and the
great pulpit. Behind the pulpit was a large cross cut into the
marble and concrete. "You see this cross?" the pastor asked.
"Yes," we replied, "it is beautiful." "Well, during the
time the church was closed and turned into a school, the
authorities took cement and covered the cross. They
reasoned that since no one could see it, no one would know
about it." Then the pastor, taking a deep breath and breaking

into a big smile said with profound conviction: "We knew it was there all the time!" The message we are called to proclaim is eternal. We witness to a kingdom that shall never end. We take the stand to tell the story of Jesus and the love of God for all creation.

Perhaps we could be accused of overemphasizing the content of the testimony; however, as Sir Alan Walker has often pointed out, "What shall it profit the church, if it perfects its technique and discovers it has nothing to say?"

We praise God that we do have something to say! And we stake our very lives on the conviction that God did, in fact, come in human form in Jesus Christ to redeem creation, including all people everywhere. What a message we have to tell to a desperate world! Surely the redeemed of the Lord are constrained to say so. "For the love of Christ urges us on" (2 Cor. 5:14).

Chapter Six

The Gospel Demands a Response

P reaching and testifying presuppose an invitation. When the gospel is proclaimed, the invitation is imperative. This is why the recommended order of worship in most hymnals includes an invitation to Christian discipleship. However, this aspect of Christian worship has been so neglected and so abused that it needs careful and prayerful consideration.

Preaching and testifying always have a purpose, and the purpose relates to the response being sought from the hearers. In our definition of preaching and testifying (see chapter two), we insisted that they are an act of proclaiming the biography of the deeds of God, in light of our autobiography, with the desire that persons, enabled by the Holy Spirit, respond to God's act of forgiveness in Jesus Christ in repentance and faith and live out the new life in faithfulness to the kingdom of God. In this chapter we will see why this response is necessary and what the response involves in terms of compassion and integrity.

When asked, "Why preach and testify for response?" the most direct answer is simply, "Because of the content of the gospel." The invitation to Christian discipleship is inherent in the gospel. This is why worship is incomplete without an invitation to respond. Paul Hoon indicates that this rhythm of God's act and human response is the cornerstone of the meaning of worship as encounter. Hoon insists that worship has integrity only as it sets before persons the decision of faith.[18]

Because the call to respond is part of the essence of the gospel, the early apostles were not shy about asking people to decide for or against the God who had already decided for them.[19] The apostles first proclaimed the deeds of salvation that put humankind right with God, and then they challenged persons to respond to this gift of forgiveness. It was natural for the hearers to inquire, "What shall we do to be saved?" The response that was sought was repentance, faith, and baptism. The early apostles understood the dynamic that makes it necessary for an offered gift to be accepted in order for it to be appropriated in the receiver's life. The gospel, of its very nature, is a knock at the door that claims attention and demands response.

In an early period of the church's history, Justin Martyr described the worship of the early church at Rome. He indicated that there were readings of the Prophets and Epistles that were followed by exhortation. Persons were instructed, encouraged, and invited to respond to the admonitions in the scripture lections by practicing these truths. This invitation to practice the truths was followed by prayers of faith together in the community and concluded by the receiving of the bread and cup. Thus, we see how the rhythm of proclamation and response in worship was practiced by the early church.[20]

Doctrine of the Word of God

The necessity for response inherent in the gospel can be seen especially in terms of our doctrine of the Word of God. The ordination ritual for The Methodist Church says, "Be thou a faithful dispenser of the Word of God." Again, it says, "Take thou authority to preach the Word of God." Accordingly, it is the Word of God that we are authorized to declare, and it is the Word of God to which we are to bear testimony (Acts 8:25).

But, what is meant by *Word of God*? Surely, we do not mean mere words or gibberish! Fundamentally, *Word of God* means the activity of God in history. The God of the Bible acts, and the story of God's dealing with us and all creation, which is the drama of redemption, becomes God's Word. Because the prophets saw and understood what God was doing, they heard and proclaimed what God was saying.

Paul Scherer, a former professor at Princeton, says, "In the speaking was the acting . . . in the acting was the speaking. . . . From start to finish the biblical writers are concerned first and foremost with the mighty and saving acts of God. . . . When Isaiah and Jeremiah tell of what God has done and will do, they are more than interpreters of some event; they are the heralds of a Word which itself fashions the event. To speak of the God who acts, which was what they understood preaching (and testifying) to be, was for them one of those acts."[21]

We have already noted that it is God's action in history to which we give testimony. God's action began in creation and creation is the first expression of God's grace. Obviously, we did not ask for creation nor did we deserve it. Moreover, God did not have to create. There was no necessity outside of God's self that forced God to create. Instead, God created because God wanted to. Creation represents the overflowing of fullness, not the hunger of emptiness. This sense of God's grace in creation becomes the foundation of all things.

What was the first thing that God did in creation? God spoke. When God spoke, creation happened. Word *became* deed. This is why Christians believe that Word has creative power.[22]

Furthermore, we see in the early chapters of Genesis how Word and deed were held together in creative balance. This creative balance is reaffirmed in the prologue to John's

Gospel. It reads: "In the beginning was the Word, and the Word was with God, and the Word was God. He was in the beginning with God. All things came into being through him, and without him not one thing came into being. And the Word became flesh" (John 1:1-3 and 14*a*). God speaks and creation happens. Word becomes deed. Word was present in creation. Word becomes flesh. God *does* by saying and *says* by doing. This is the reason Christians contend that words act and deeds speak. In a process of complementarity, word and deed are joined in creation.

It is the good news of God's action that we are authorized to proclaim. The action of God is expressed in creation, in the call of Abraham, in the liberation of Israel, in the giving of the law and covenant, in the sending of the prophets, and ultimately, "in the fullness of time" in the sending of God's own Son into the world. In the events of the birth, life, ministry, death, resurrection, and ascension of Jesus, as well as in the gift of the Holy Spirit at Pentecost, God's salvation is made manifest and the church of Jesus Christ is born.

Earlier, we saw how God's Word has creative power. This fundamental truth has crucial implications for preaching and testifying. In a mysterious and creative way, word and deed come together in preaching and testimony. P. T. Forsyth once said, "The Gospel (or Good News) is an eternal, perennial act of God in Christ repeating itself within each declaration of it. . . . It is this act that is prolonged in the words of the preacher and not merely proclaimed. . . . A true sermon is a real deed."[23] A perennial flower is one that keeps coming up season after season. In gospel witnessing, God's act in Christ is repeated again and again and made available for the hearer. This act of God in Christ is *prolonged* in the words of the proclaimer and not merely proclaimed.

In preaching and testimony, God is making God's saving activity available to the people. Here we are dealing with a profound sacramental mystery. In preaching and testifying the ordinary words spoken by ordinary people are baptized by the Holy Spirit and become the means for the real presence of our Lord Jesus Christ. In the words of the proclaimer, the Word of God is made manifest. This is why we believe that the Word has creative power.

The great D. T. Niles once said, "Words make things happen. One person speaking to another involves far more than mere sounds being created and transmitted and heard. It is more like arrows or bullets being shot into a given place. Spoken words are units of energy. They go out to do things and make a difference in the realities they touch. Words are a form of deed."[24] Because of this conviction, John Claypool was led to define proclamation as an "event." He says, "Word is every bit as decisive a deed as an act of the hand or an act of the foot. Words are power. . . ."[25]

These truths have led us to the conviction that there is an "event-content" to Christian communication. The content of our proclamation is not an affirmation of ideas that people must practice; it is not an explanation of life and its problems about which we may argue. Rather, it is the announcement of events with which people must reckon. Our doctrine of the Word of God teaches us that the fundamental ground of witnessing is a good news event that must be proclaimed and to which people must respond.

According to our faith, an extraordinary event that came at the peak of a whole process of revelation has changed and is changing the whole context of human living—the event of God in the birth, life, ministry, death, ascension, and resurrection of Jesus Christ. Our responsibility is to allow this action of God to transform us as we open our lives to God's creative power. Then, our responsibility is to live in terms of this salvation-event, celebrate this key event, proclaim this event, and invite all others to do likewise. In the proclamation of this good news event God discloses God's self and beckons us to respond.

When this Word of God, this event-content, this good news is faithfully presented, it carries with it a power all its own. The apostle Paul said, "For I am not ashamed of the gospel; it is the power of God for salvation to everyone who has faith" (Rom. 1:16). Notice, the power is in the gospel and not in the gospel messenger. It is the good news content of Christian preaching and testimony that elicits response. The Word of God has its own way of addressing the human soul. Therefore, the gospel is not so utterly dependent on us as we are sometimes inclined to believe.

According to Paul, it is the gospel on which we stand and through which we are being saved (1 Cor. 15:1-2). The gospel has a power all its own, and we do not have to put power into it. Dietrich Bonhoeffer affirms this truth: "It is wrong to suppose that there is a Word on the one hand and a church on the other, and that it is the task of the preacher to take that Word into his hands and move it so as to bring it into the church and apply it to the church's needs. On the contrary, the Word moves of its own accord, and all the preacher has to do is assist that movement and try to put no obstacles in its path."[26]

We remember how mountain preachers would stand at the pulpit, read their text, drop to their knees and pray, "Lord, hide me behind the cross and do not allow me to get in the way of what you wish to do here." Their theology was not very sophisticated, but their practice certainly was in keeping with Bonhoeffer's admonition that we are to assist the movement of the Word and try not to put any obstacles in its path. The proclaimer's responsibility is to get the message straight, get to the heart of the matter, and get the message out as often as possible.

Often, our failure to get to the heart of the matter results in putting obstacles in the path of the gospel. Dr. Albert C. Outler, speaking to the Uniting Conference of The United

Methodist Church in 1968, gave a wonderful summary of
the heart of the gospel:

> The church is called to mission, and her mission is both her
> message and the demonstration of that message in her
> corporate life. Her message is not *herself* either—it is her
> witness to the Christian Evangel: To the scandal and folly of
> Christ incarnate, Christ crucified, Christ resurrected, Christ
> transforming human life and culture, Christ in the world;
> Christ in us, our hope of glory! Thus, the church we are called
> to be must be truly evangelical—a church ablaze with a passion
> that God's gospel shall be preached and heard and responded
> to in faith and hope and love by all who can be reached and
> instructed and gathered into the fellowship of God's coven-
> anted people. The fullness of the gospel embraces all human
> concerns everywhere and always; but the heart of the gospel is
> startlingly simple: That God loves you and me and all persons
> with a very special love and that Jesus Christ is the sufficient
> proof of that love to any person who will receive and confess
> Him as Savior and Lord.

When we get to the heart of the message, the message has a
power all its own.

As we have seen, the message of the early church was
thoroughly Christ-centered. They proclaimed Jesus. When
Philip joined the carriage of the Ethiopian Eunuch, he began
with the Old Testament passage the Eunuch was reading,
then he proceeded to testify to the "good news about Jesus"
(Acts 8:35). Jesus Christ was presented as the fulfillment of
God's work in history. He was presented as the beginning of a
new era in terms of people's relationships with God, one
another, and all creation. Jesus, the man, the crucified one,
the risen one, the exalted one, the returning one; Jesus the
present one in the power of the Spirit—Jesus was the core of
their preaching and testifying. Moreover, they offered the
gift of forgiveness, adoption, reconciliation, and the gift of

the Holy Spirit. Finally, they looked for a response. As we said earlier, they were not shy about asking the people to decide for or against the gospel. They expected results and God honored their faith and expectation.

Not only does this good news event carry with it a power all its own, it carries with it a demand for response. You either accept it, reject it, postpone it, or reduce it, but you must respond. In other words, implicit in the message is a call to Christian discipleship. Therefore, the invitation to Christian discipleship is not only theologically appropriate, it is absolutely necessary. This basic conviction led the late Bishop Harold Heininger to say, "It is immoral to preach the gospel and not give an invitation, and it is immoral to give an invitation without preaching the gospel." This seems a rather harsh thing to say! Why would this leader of the church and gifted homiletician make such an assertion?

We are sure that the answer to this question lies somewhere in the difference between knowledge of Christianity and knowledge of Christ. These forms of knowledge are qualitatively different. Knowledge of Christianity depends on one's level of education, culture, and one's native intelligence. But, knowledge of Christ depends on love, reverence, obedience, and trust. The first form of knowledge—knowledge of Christianity—depends more on intellectual concepts or propositions. But, the second form—knowledge of Christ—depends on personal relationship or encounter.

As we have said, God is disclosed in the gospel when this gospel appears as indwelling Spirit in the life of the communicator and is articulated in word and deed. Knowledge *about* God can be transmitted through books and tracts but the personal knowledge *of* God is communicated through a vital, living testimony of self-revelation.

Confrontation with God's self-disclosure in the gospel is what we mean by an encounter that demands response. Emil

Brunner called this "truth as encounter" and says, "In the Bible there encounters us now as formerly, the truth of the God who came, is present, and will come to man (sic). Faith is kindled, not by theology, but by the Word of God, by the history of the God who proclaims Himself and gives us a part with Himself."[27]

To receive this powerful communication from God is not to receive a piece of information about God, but to receive *God*. Again Brunner affirms: "In his Word, God does not deliver to me a course of lectures in dogmatic theology, God does not submit to me or interpret for me the content of a confession of faith, but he makes himself accessible to me. . . . He does not communicate something to me, but himself. God is a person who himself speaks and discloses himself . . . an exchange takes place here which is wholly without analogy in the sphere of thinking. The sole analogy is in the encounter between human beings, the meeting of person with person."[28]

The geographer can transmit a knowledge of geography, a chemist of chemistry, a mathematician of mathematics. Knowledge of persons, human or divine, is a gift of grace, which only persons can give. This gift of grace depends on personal relationship or encounter. The sole analogy is in the encounter between human beings, the meeting of person with person. It is an I–Thou, not an I–it situation.

Martin Buber tells how he has often sat at his desk with books and papers before him, if not master, then at least manager in the realm of things; when all at once the telephone rings and a voice which he has never confused with any other voice says, "Martin, dinner is ready." In an instant the whole situation is transformed because a higher order of reality has cut across his existence. What is called for now is not so much reason as response to encounter and relationship.[29]

So it is with the Christian gospel. It is more than a message; it is more than catechism; it is more than a system of intellectual thought; the Christian gospel is a message with a Messenger. Through the gospel, God is made accessible to us. Christian communication, therefore, evokes a discovery situation, a disclosure situation, a John 3:19 situation, when the light of truth breaks through and people must choose between darkness and light. In the teaching of Paul, since God has already said, *Yes* to us in the person of Christ Jesus, we are challenged to meet God's divine Yes with our own "yes" (2 Cor. 1:19-20).

When a person testifies to the gospel, that person is posing a yes-or-no situation. There are situations that demand a yes-or-no. These situations usually involve personal relationships: Such as when a man says to a woman, "Darling, I love you. Will you marry me?" This is a yes-or-no situation. She can say "yes" or she can say "no," but if she gives no answer at all, she is actually saying "no." The question is posed as a moment of truth and at such a moment the person must respond. When the preacher or lay witness invites response, it is because he or she believes that at that moment there is a moment of truth that demands a yes-or-no answer.

Therefore, the proclaimer's business is not to ask, "Shall I preach and testify for a response or a verdict?" The doctrine of the Word of God teaches us that that question is theologically illegitimate. The preacher or lay witness should be saying, "God, help me to witness so that there may be a disclosure of the truth in Christ." That's what preaching and testifying are all about. We are leading our hearers into a discovery situation—when truth becomes luminous. In such a moment and in such a situation, the verdict is demanded not so much by the proclaimer but by the power of truth that comes through the gospel.

The invitation is within the disclosure. It is the God of the disclosure who is doing the inviting. The preacher or lay witness only cooperates with the nature of the truth disclosed and tries not to put any obstacles in its path. The apostle Paul speaks forcefully on this issue: "All this is from God, who reconciled us to himself through Christ, and has given us the ministry of reconciliation; that is, in Christ God was reconciling the world to himself, not counting their trespasses against them, and entrusting the message of reconciliation to us. So we are ambassadors for Christ, since God is making his appeal through us; we entreat you on behalf of Christ, be reconciled to God" (2 Cor. 5:18-21). *God appeals through us.*

To put it another way, the proclaimer's responsibility is to enable the hearers to let God's disclosure be a live option and to say an authentic "yes" or "no" to God. Therefore, the messenger attempts to bring the hearers to the point where the message is in the forefront of their consciousness, so they can struggle with the living God. What an awesome task! It's no wonder that the mountain preachers would pray, "Lord, hide me behind the cross and do not let me get in the way of what you want to do." David H. C. Read says, "This proclamation of a life-changing Word that demands a decision has lain at the heart of the Christian gospel from the beginning. It is the enduring mystery that through words spoken and heard the story of Jesus comes alive in such a way as to elicit an allegiance to him as Savior and Lord."[30]

God's Word is *Event* that creates reality, *Action* that obliges involvement, and a *Person* who cannot be ignored. When the redeemed of the Lord say so, they declare the Word of God—the gospel. It carries with it a creative power all its own and it demands response.

The Context for Preaching and Testifying

Chapter Seven

Hearing the People's Cry

O ften our failure to be effective witnesses is occasioned not so much by lack of understanding of the content of the gospel or any lack of confidence in the power of the gospel, but rather a failure in our ability to discern the context for preaching and testifying. Therefore, we now give attention to perceiving the situation of the hearers.

Preaching and testifying are for the people's sake. There are many people in the world who are hurting and know what it is to live their lives in bondage. Those who go forth to preach and testify have heard not only the call of God, they have also heard the cry of the people. In London we watched the famous musical *Les Miserables*. It is the story of the oppression and suffering of the people just prior to the French Revolution. We were deeply moved by a gripping scene in which the words echoed again and again, "Can you hear the people? Can you hear the people crying? Can you hear the people singing?" The musical gave a poignant portrayal of human misery and oppression that overwhelms us. Charles Wesley, like his brother John, was finally compelled to speak in the open air because he was haunted by the faces of thousands of helpless people who were in bondage without the saving knowledge of Jesus Christ. For the people's sake, the Wesleys heard the people cry and were propelled outward

into the streets of industrial cities and mining towns. The
Wesleys were following the example of Jesus, who ministered
for the people's sake.

As one reads the New Testament, one is confronted again
and again with texts that illustrate the compassion of Jesus.
When Jesus saw the rich young ruler in bondage to his
possessions, he was moved with compassion, "Jesus, looking
at him, loved him" (Mark 10:21). He said to the woman who
had suffered from hemorrhages for twelve years and had
touched the hem of his garment, "Daughter, your faith has
made you well; go in peace" (Luke 8:48). While passing
through Jericho, Jesus, in compassion, turned toward the
lonely tax collector Zacchaeus and said, "Zacchaeus, hurry
and come down; for I must stay at your house today" (Luke
19:5). Upon his triumphal entry into Jerusalem when he
"came near and saw the city, he wept over it" (Luke 19:41).
When Jesus confronted the great crowds he had compassion
"because they were like sheep without a shepherd; and he
began to teach them many things" (Mark 6:34). Jesus sees,
feels, and hears the cries of the people. Anyone who follows
Jesus must not only see the people but must also hear their
cries. Seeing and hearing are prerequisites for understanding
context and for compassionate action.

The Context of the Message

The necessity of understanding context is in keeping with
the historical nature of the Christian faith. Jesus, John the
Baptist, and all the prophets in the Old Testament were
called at particular times to a particular people in order to
articulate a particular message. Of Isaiah it is said that "In the
year that King Uzziah died, I saw the Lord" (Isa. 6:1). Of
Jeremiah, it is said "the word of the Lord came in the days of
King Josiah" (Jer. 1:2). Of Daniel it is said, "In the third year
of the reign of King Belshazzar a vision appeared" (Dan. 8:1).
The ministry of John the Baptist is said to have happened "In

the fifteenth year of the reign of Emperor Tiberius, when Pontius Pilate was governor of Judea" (Luke 3:1). Of Jesus it is said his birth happened when "Quirinius was governor of Syria" (Luke 2:2).

The point of all of this is that the revelations of God are never divorced from time. Likewise, preaching and testifying can never be divorced from time because the gospel of the kingdom attains its meaning in and through history. In the Book of Acts we see how the early Christian witnesses took their historical context with utter seriousness. This delivered them from the crippling uniformity that is often the burden of today's church. As we have seen, there was a basic content to their apostolic witness, but there was wide diversity in terms of the ways in which they made their message known. Most of the variety in the testifying and preaching found in the New Testament is evoked because of radically different contexts, differences in gospel advocates and the ways in which these advocates perceived the needs of the people.

The particular way in which God speaks to particular people through particular people at particular times and in particular places is so important in the history of revelation that it constitutes a controlling principle in preaching and testifying. Thus, in the verbal communication of the gospel the witness must constantly ask four critical contextual questions:

First, to whom am I bringing the gospel? It is clear that Paul took a different approach to communication with Festus and Agrippa (Acts 26) than he did when he stood before the crowd at Lystra (Acts 14), Athens (Acts 17) or Ephesus (Acts 19).

Second, we must ask, what person brings the gospel? Elisha is different from Elijah. Matthew presents the gospel in a somewhat different form than does John. The settings in which the advocates of the gospel are born, their sex, development, cultural background, personality characteris-

tics, and age all play a part and are used by God in making the
gospel known.

Third, those who preach and testify must continually ask,
"What is the timing for the divine-human encounter? Is the
harvest ready?" Each historical moment has its own dynamic
opportunities and responsibilities, as well as blockages and
difficulties. The one who witnesses must remain continuously
open to the inspiration of the Holy Spirit, for it is the Holy
Spirit who sensitizes us, enabling us to discern God's timing
and the receptivity of the people. Urgency regarding our
witnessing is inseparably linked with urgency relating to the
harvest. When "the fields are ripe for harvesting," that is no
time for the "reaper" to hold back (John 4:35)! Without the
inspiration of the Holy Spirit we stumble into the harvest
either when the crop is premature or else bent over by winter
storms and rotting in the rows.

Finally, when we attempt to preach and testify we must
constantly ask, "What are the realities of the place in which
we are sent to witness?" Knowledge of our missional territory
is critical to every form of missionary work.

It is amazing how little we know about the people in our
territory, especially those people who are outside the church.
Sometimes our failure to communicate the gospel is not
because we fail to know the story, it is because we do not know
the people.

On one occasion, when one of the authors was visiting with
a pastor in another city he asked, "What is that building there
near your church?" He replied, "It is a school. Yes. I think it is
a school." When asked, "What kind of school?" He replied, "I
don't know." This pastor was completely oblivious to a whole
community of people within a stone's throw of his church. He
did not even know the ages of the children attending the
school.

It is simply astonishing how little some of us know about
our own missional territory. The authors have informally

conducted surveys among pastors and church lay leaders over the years by asking the question: "Tell me about the ministry of your church." Nine out of ten, respond by telling about the church in terms of membership, attendance, budget, structures, committees, and so forth. Very seldom does a church leader start out describing the community, the territory, or the people in the area where the church building is located.

If the church is to bear witness to those people in the world who have little or no relationship with the church, the church must turn around and face the world. For the world does not exist for the sake of the church, the church exists for the sake of the world. And people do not exist for the sake of the Sabbath, the Sabbath exists for the sake of the people (Mark 2:27).

We have a tendency to turn away from our primary place of ministry and become preoccupied with secondary venues. Bishops turn away from the annual conference to the general church. District superintendents and pastors turn away from the district and congregation in response to the gravitational pull of the conference. Laypeople turn away from their responsibility to witness in the world and become occupied with "church work." The church tends to turn from mission to maintenance. If we are to be the evangelistic movement God is calling us to be, the whole system must turn around and face the world. John Wesley declared the "world is my parish." Today, the parish has become our world. In the tendency to turn away from the world and face inward, the church greatly neglects its evangelistic mandate: "Go into all the world, and proclaim the good news to the whole creation" (Mark 16:15).

The commission is to penetrate the world with the gospel of the kingdom. When the church becomes nearsighted and turns in on itself, it loses its compassion and surrenders its reason for being. It resembles more the Fortress Zion than that first-century dynamic movement of the Spirit that spread like wildfire across the Roman empire and the known world. The hymn writer, Samuel Wolcott, sees the vision of what God intends for the church:

> Christ for the world we sing, the world to Christ we bring, with loving zeal; the poor, and them that mourn, the faint and over borne, sin sick and sorrow worn, whom Christ doth heal.

> Christ for the world we sing, the world to Christ we bring, with fervent prayer; the wayward and the lost, by restless passions tossed, redeemed at countless cost, from dark despair.

> Christ for the world we sing, the world to Christ we bring with one accord; with us the work to share, with us reproach to dare, with us the cross to bear, for Christ our Lord.

> Christ for the world we sing, the world to Christ we bring, with joyful song; the newborn souls, whose days, reclaimed from error's ways, inspired with hope and praise, to Christ belong.

"Christ for the World We Sing" targets the whole world. The Holy Spirit empowers witnesses to witness not only in Jerusalem, Judea, and Samaria but even to the ends of the earth (Acts 1:8).

Where Does Witnessing Begin?

Witnessing always begins at home. In order to fulfill this mandate, it is necessary for the church to be able to discern the immediate realities that serve as the framework for the communication of the gospel. Do we know the people in our territory?

A church was debating the type of building it should erect. Should it build a sanctuary for worship or a family-life center for education? The building committee suggested that the church should survey its members and discover what the members wanted. But some of the committee resisted, saying, "No, we should ask not what do our members want, but what does this community need?" Whereupon, the church set out to learn all it could about its community.

When the church requested information from the Government Census Bureau about the area in which the church was located, the bureau was amazed and said, "Churches do not ordinarily ask for this information. Those who come most often for this type of information are from McDonald's." Before they build, the McDonald's Corporation knows how many people will eat their hamburgers and how many are available for employment. They make it a point to know the community because the life of the business depends on it. What a pity that the people who sell hamburgers know more about the realities of the community than those whose primary mission is to bear witness to the gospel. Is it any wonder that many churches are lapsing into a maintenance mode rather than becoming vital congregations alive with faithful disciples? The time has come for us to give an accounting of our stewardship of the gospel and our responsibility to the world.

Who are the people in your place? The important question is not the size of your church building or the number in your congregation, but rather, how many persons are in your village, neighborhood, city, or area who have yet to know the liberating good news of Jesus? To those who would dare preach and testify, the call is to turn around and face the realities of the place in which we minister.

Understanding the Culture

If one is serious about preaching and testifying, one must not only know the realities of the place, but must also discern the people and the culture. A people's cultural values are expressed through song, art, story, literature, dance, and other customs and traditions by which people establish and define their identity. The world is characterized by a variety of cultural identities. For the most part these various cultural expressions are primarily different, rather than being superior and inferior.

The Southern Appalachian region of the United States, where the authors grew up, has its own cultural identity and expression. To one who is an outsider (a person who has not lived in the region for at least three or four generations) the people of Appalachia are peculiar. If a person from outside the region moves into an Appalachian community, the people will sometimes treat that person as an outsider. This makes the witness wonder what is wrong with himself or herself. If the witness indicates that the people's music and language are inadequate, it makes the people wonder if they are inferior.

It is important for those who preach and testify to realize that people are different, but not necessarily superior or inferior. Without this realization, cultural imperialism can be practiced against people. This happens most often when those who witness fail to take seriously the language and culture of the people. If it were not so serious, our attempts to communicate with each other would be somewhat humorous. Many forms of communication are culturally defined— shaking hands, bowing to one another, hugging one another, kissing the other person, or nodding to the individual. If we are to take other people seriously, it is absolutely necessary that we know the cultural forms of those to whom we are witnessing.

Sometimes we, the authors, have felt that both lay and clergy witnesses should receive training in cross-cultural communication. Our exposure to a variety of cultures outside the United States has reinforced this need. Moreover, the increasing pluralism of North America is giving this need a new place of prominence. From personal experience we have seen how cultural realities can either serve as bridges or blinders in the communication of the gospel.

All attempts at witnessing to the gospel are culture-bound. In other words, each and every presentation of the gospel is given with a very particular and distinct accent. No presentation can be freed from the influences of time, history, and culture. How could it be otherwise? Time, history, personality characteristics, and cultural realities are the milieu in which the revelations of God happen. This should not be considered as a handicap or a negative factor. It is merely an outgrowth of the Christian's most basic conviction: "And the Word became flesh and lived among us" (John 1:14). The trouble comes when the witness fails to recognize the peculiar cultural garments in which his or her presentation of the gospel is clothed, or even worse, when the witness assumes that his or her particular cultural garments are an integral part of the gospel itself. Then it is that evangelization becomes a cruel and insensitive form of cultural imperialism.

We have seen the devastating effects this has on the people. Often this happens without any insidious design or intent on the part of the advocate. Unfortunately, one can become so "pickled" in one's own language and culture that it is almost impossible to discern and positively affirm a language and culture that is radically different. The ability to become all things to all people in order to win some is a divine gift of the Holy Spirit.

Paul exemplified this divine gift in his life, ministry, and writings. To the church at Corinth he wrote:

> For though I am free with respect to all, I have made myself a slave to all, so that I might win more of them. To the Jews I became as a Jew, in order to win Jews. To those under the law I became as one under the law (though I myself am not under the law) so that I might win those under the law. To those outside the law I became as one outside the law (though I am not free from God's law but am under Christ's law) so that I might win those outside the law. To the weak I became weak, so that I might win the weak. I have become all things to all people, that

I might by all means save some. I do it all for the sake of the
gospel, so that I may share in its blessings. (1 Cor. 9:19-23)

It is extremely difficult to place oneself in solidarity with
someone else's culture or situation. Nonetheless, Paul makes
it clear that we are called to do so in order to relate with others
in such a way that effective dialogue and proclamation are
possible. Like Paul, we do it all for the sake of the gospel. Paul
faithfully proclaimed the gospel without ignoring the cultural
realities and situations of the people.

Anyone who yearns to be a faithful bearer of truth must
recognize the value of people and their ways of living. This
creates tension within us. It is the ancient conflict in Christian
evangelization of how to be *in* the world but not *of* it.
Sometimes the values of the culture are in direct conflict with
the reality of the reign of God. For example, there is no hint of
bondage in original creation and God's rule, but our world is
one which seeks to dominate and enslave others. The great
power brokers wish to usurp the reign of God and impose
their will over the oppressed and powerless. Wherever this is
a part of cultural realities it cannot be blessed or condoned. It
must be denounced and transformed.

In addition, culture always seeks to capture Christ and at
the same time receive the blessing of the reign of God.
Accordingly, many in the church wish to strip Jesus of his
messianic authority, empty him of his sense of mission, and
fill him with notions and ideologies that fit their own cause.
Thus Jesus becomes a guerrilla fighter or "Rambo" fighting
for someone's cause, ideology, or ambition. This "captive
Christ" can be stripped of his seamless robe and wrapped in
the hood of the Ku Klux Klan. He can be dressed in the
three-piece suit of a selfish capitalist, or he can be shoved
before a television camera to endorse all sorts of ideas and
fads. This captive Christ can be conscripted and issued the

ill-fitting uniform of almost any nation or group fighting for almost any cause.[1]

The gospel has the power to transform and reconcile that which is contrary to the reign of God. In one of our visits to the beautiful island of Fiji we were invited to see the ancient island of the chief, Bau Island. This tiny island has a magnificent view of the South Pacific. On the island is a small, attractive Methodist chapel. Inside the chapel, we were shown a large stone approximately three feet high and two feet wide. On the top of the stone was a small indentation. We were told this stone was used in ancient times to crush the heads of the children of captives before they were eaten by the cannibal natives. Today, the same stone is used to hold water for the baptism of children! What was once a symbol of death is now an expression of grace and life.

The gospel always holds our cultures and its values under judgment, and always the gospel is seeking to transform culture in terms of the reign of God. Thus when Christians pray, "Thy Kingdom come, thy will be done, on earth as it is in heaven," wherever they are, whatever their culture, they are pleading for a radical transformation to happen.

The limited scope of this book, as well as the limitation of its writers, makes it both unwise and impossible to attempt any comprehensive analysis of the varieties of cultures in our vast world. Perhaps this is a good thing. The most penetrating analyses are usually those done by persons from within their own cultures. The Christian faith must take root and grow in the indigenous soil of various cultures. We can learn from one another. Many of our insights are transportable. Each witness, however, must do his or her own homework under the inspiration and guidance of the Holy Spirit. In the final analysis, it is the Holy Spirit who enables us to discern the needs of the people, hear their cries, and respond with the good news of the gospel. When the redeemed of the Lord see and hear the cry of the people they must speak and act.

Chapter Eight

Organizing the Message

I n order to communicate effectively in various contexts how do we organize our message to present the gospel story? In this chapter, we will attempt to be as practical as possible. We have been influenced by Dr. Lawrence Lacour, who has faithfully and effectively proclaimed the gospel for half a century. During his doctoral studies at Northwestern University, Lacour became convinced that the use of communication theory could greatly enhance the communication of the gospel. He believed that since the witness has the truth of the gospel on his or her side, it is all the more necessary to be open to communicating that truth as effectively as possible.

In communication theory a message that is primarily focused for response is called a speech for persuasion. Dr. Lacour utilized the research of Allen Monroe, whose fertile mind gave us the famous *motivated sequence*. Monroe believed that there is a natural sequence that the advocate must follow in order to effectively organize a persuasive address. Lacour "baptized" Monroe's Five-step Sequence and employed it to communicating the gospel. These steps may help communicators become more effective in preaching and testifying.

Attention

The opening sentence is critical to the whole message. The first sentence of a testimony or sermon is vitally important as a means of securing attention. The only thing worse than a speaker who does not know how to land, is one who does not know how to take off! Some speakers wander in circles and finally get on the proper runway and take off. The audience gets impatient and loses interest. Earlier, we observed that there is a built-in suspicion to verbal communication. This, coupled with an exceedingly brief attention span, makes it unlikely that people will wait for a speaker who wanders all over the landscape before taking off. The audience is apt to change the channel and tune the speaker out. To communicate the gospel effectively, we must quickly captivate people's interest.

Try tape-recording your testimony or sermon. Afterward, carefully listen again and again to the first sentence or paragraph. Does it grab the attention of the people? Pray and reflect on what God would want to be said first.

Need

Once you have secured their attention, begin at the point of the hearer's basic needs. To communicate the message of the kingdom, Jesus began with the situation of the hearer. It is important to realize that Jesus never pandered to people's selfish wants. This would have meant compromising the demands of the kingdom. To the contrary, he always aimed his message so as to address the basic needs of people. If we begin where our listeners are, we can demonstrate how the gospel meets their need. This is accomplished by standing in the other person's shoes and empathizing with the hearer.

Charles Wesley, the great Methodist hymn writer, wrote about six thousand hymns. The hymn texts were profoundly biblical and theological, but the hymn tunes were set to the popular music of the pubs of his day. He knew the wisdom of starting where the people were. People accepted the treasure of the gospel because the vessel that carried it was familiar. Truth must be perceived as a part of the real world of the listener if they are to give attention to that truth.

Jesus did not approach two individuals in exactly the same manner. Someone has said, "He never practiced Xerox evangelism!" His message was adapted to meet the needs of each person he encountered. He said to Nicodemus, a religious official interested in spiritual matters, "No one can see the kingdom of God without being born from above" (John 3:3). To the thirsty woman at the well he said, "Give me a drink," and proceeded to offer living water (John 4). Simon Peter, the sort of man who responds to big challenges, heard Jesus say, "Follow me and I will make you fish for people" (Mark 1:17). This invitation offered a challenge bigger than Peter had ever known. To Zacchaeus, short in stature, ostracized and lonely, Jesus said, "I must stay at your house" (Luke 19:5).

In order to make his message known Jesus always began from the perspective of the hearer. Those of us who preach and testify need a point of contact, a bridge over which truth can travel. This can be discovered through empathetic sensitivity to people's basic needs.

Empathy is an incarnational word that denotes the attempt to stand in the other person's shoes or follow in their bare footprints. This is extremely difficult, but the Holy Spirit enables one to imagine what it would be like to be the hearers listening to the message. We dare to offer a very practical exercise aimed at developing empathetic skills. In preparing a sermon or testimony, it is helpful to sincerely ask one or more of the following questions:

What is it like to be confined to a wheelchair?
What is it like to be sixteen years old?

What is it like not be invited to the party?

What is it like to be hungry?

What is it like to have a child born with a handicapping condition?

What is it like to be unemployed?

What is it like to face a malpractice suit?

What is it like to be told you are no longer needed?

What is it like to lose your "nest egg"?

What is it like to lose a friend to a drunk driver?

What is it like to lose a spouse?

What is it like to fail the entrance exam?

What is it like to fail the bar exam?

What is it like to not make the team?

What is it like to win the prize?

What is it like to lose the tournament?

What is it like to have to learn Braille?

What is it like to live on the streets?

What is it like to stand in a bread line?

What is it like to live under an oppressive regime?

What is it like to scrounge for food on a garbage dump?

What is it like to always breathe polluted air?

What is it like to live next door to a nuclear plant?

What is it like to lose the family farm after five generations?

What is it like to have AIDS?

What is it like to discover your spouse is having an affair?

What is it like to lose everything in a financial crash?

What is it like to be impotent?

What is it like to suffer the pain of divorce?

What is it like when your children disappoint you?

What is it like to be abused as a child?

What is it like to be a conscientious objector?

What is it like to live in a refugee camp?

What is it like to be a battered woman?

What is it like to be the slowest learner?

What is it like to always be chosen last for the team?

What is it like to be faithful to Christ in Australia? in England? in the USA? in India? in Thailand? in Lebanon? in Israel? in Brazil? in Nigeria? in China?

What is it like to be rejected by your family because you follow Jesus?

What is it like to be overweight?

What is it like to discover the illness is terminal?

What is it like to be in prison?

What is it like to be compelled to fight for your country?

If we dare speak from the perspective of the hearer, we must attempt to sit where they sit and think and feel as they do.

Announcing Good News

Once we have made contact with the hearers' basic need, we announce the good news. The word that denotes evangelizing comes from a Greek term meaning "bringing the good message." The Greek term *euangellion* is a compound word. The prefix "eu" means good. We see this in such words as "euphoria." Anytime a Greek word carries the "eu" prefix, it means that something is good. The opposite of the "eu" word is a "dys" word. "Dys" means that something is definitely bad. You see this in such words as "dysentery." Much of what goes under the name of evangelism could best be called "dysangelism"—bad news.

In a world that tends to be preoccupied with bad news, people hunger to hear a good word from God. Therefore, we must ask the question, Where is the good news in this message? Especially, where is the good news for these particular people?

We recall a member of a former congregation who suffered a complete mental and emotional breakdown. After diagnosing her case, the psychiatrist remarked to the family, "She is suffering from an overload of bad news and doesn't seem to be able to find a way to shelter herself against it."

The media are constantly bombarding the public with bad news and there does not seem to be a way to escape it. If people hear only bad news from the witness, they find themselves having to accept a stone and/or snake rather than the bread of life (Matt. 7:9). Every sermon and testimony must undergo a "good news test." The advocate must ask, "Is the good news of God's love, grace, and righteous reign explicitly present in my message?"

Visualization

After gaining attention and speaking the good news in terms of basic human needs, it is important to visualize the main points of the message. Preaching and testifying are basically visual. Jesus did not list thirty-two systematic reasons why we should believe in the kingdom of God. To the contrary, he said, "The kingdom of God is like . . . ." He couched the truth in visual images familiar to his hearers. He spoke of the pearl of great price, treasure in a field, seeds, sowers, and harvest; of vineyards, sheep, shepherds, salt, and light; of children, fathers, mothers, flowers, birds, stewards, and masters; of banquets, weddings, parties, bread, and wine; and of sunsets, wind, sea, fish, fishermen, nets, and yeast. He was able to help his hearers visualize what the kingdom is like. Visualization enables the hearers to understand the truth and apply it to their own lives.

Martin Luther King, Jr., was a master at employing the art of visualization. This art is illustrated again and again in his speaking, but the best illustration was his message "I Have a Dream" presented in Washington, D.C. After securing the rapt attention of his audience, highlighting the needs of the hour, and demonstrating how the gospel addressed those needs, King dramatized his message by thundering, "I have a dream."

King spoke of a day forthcoming when the little white boy and the little black boy would walk hand in hand together across this land. By the time he finished his message, millions of people began to dream with him. Many of those persons could not state an infallible rationale as to why the races should live together, but nevertheless, they had caught a vision of what racial inclusiveness would look like. From that moment forward they lived by their visions and dreams rather than being driven by their dread and fear. As a result, many were willing to risk life and limb for the sake of the cause.

Visualization enables a person to participate in history rather than allowing history to steamroll over him or her. Visualization makes people pro-active rather than re-active. This is seen in Dr. King's presentation on that fateful day in Memphis, Tennessee, when he was shot to death. Earlier that day he said, "I have been to the mountain, I haven't been to the other side but I have seen the other side." Millions of people can now say, "Yes, we see it too, and we are willing to commit ourselves to such a vision."

Joe Harding, preacher and evangelist, challenges all who preach and testify to let their "pictures" do the talking. The world is good at communicating in images. Often the world distorts the image and twists it to fit its own desired end. But over and over the images rush at us and overwhelm us. Since people are tuned to images, let the witness not be afraid to paint pictures that enable people to say, "I can *see* what you are saying."

A dear friend and colleague, the late Glenn "Tex" Evans, taught us more than we ever could imagine about the art of visualization. He was a master painter with words. The following unedited material is from an oral presentation at the national gathering of New Life Missioners (1976). It is a prime illustration of his God-given ability to visualize:

> The gospel is like Bermuda grass in east Texas. I grew up in east Texas and I know about Bermuda grass. Now, I'll tell you. If you did not grow up in east Texas and don't

know about Bermuda grass, well you need to know. I also
lived in eastern Kentucky for many years, and one time I
took two old Kentuckians down to east Texas with me
just to see where I'd come from. Knowing the
Kentuckians had made a lot of money in the sawmill
business and had done enormously well with coal
mining, they wanted to go down to east Texas to see
some of the sights down there. And I showed them a lot
of things to remember. I showed 'em some bulls,
sawmills. I showed 'em some lizards of east Texas. I
showed 'em some of those tall pine trees. Why, we've got
trees down there so tall you have to put hinges on them
in order to let 'em down at night so the moon can pass. I
showed 'em some of those trees; I showed 'em the
forests. And I showed 'em some of my relatives down
there.

I introduced them to an old friend of mine named Jeff
Waller. Jeff was a real hit with them, because over and
over again they remembered my friend Jeff Waller. They
had quite a conversation with him.

They said, "Mr. Waller, what do you do for a living?"
"Well, I'm fifty-four years old and I've lived right around
here all that time. The last fifty years I have spent my
time fighting Bermuda grass. And you can tell from most
of my clothes and my hound-dog-look how successful
I've been." They asked, "What do you mean, you've
been fighting Bermuda grass? Why do you fight
Bermuda grass?" "Well, what else can you do around
here? You can't lean against the fence all your life with
your pants held up with a ten-penny nail and a clothes
pin. You can't sit on your front porch waitin' for a lawn
mower to fall in your front yard. You've gotta do
somethin', so you fight Bermuda grass."

They asked, "Well, why do you fight Bermuda grass?"
"To kill it." Curiously they asked, "Can Bermuda grass

be killed?" He said, "Why, sure it can be killed. You see that patch right over there?" "Yes." "Well, I've killed that patch twenty-seven times—right over there." Puzzled, they asked, "If you've killed it twenty-seven times, why is it still there?" "Because it's Bermuda grass!" Waller exclaimed. He went on, "Buddy, I'm telling you right now if you ain't had the joy of fighting Bermuda grass, you don't know what a slow death is like." Then he said, "Fella, I'll tell you what you can do. You can go out in your field and dig it up, get you a plow, get you a hoe, get you a rake, get you a shovel, get all your family out there. You can dig up every blade, root, stalk, stem, and take it out to the end of the row and hang it on a barbed wire fence and it will still take root and grow on that barbed wire fence."

They said, "You don't mean it?"

"I do mean it. My neighbor Leroy Talbert has eighteen goats in that shed over there and he ain't fed 'em nothin' except that Bermuda grass hanging on my barbed wire fence. Every time it rains, it blooms and grows—that's all there is to it."

He goes on, "You can go out to your garden, and you can dig it up, stub, sprout, root and everything—dig it up and put it into a nice, neat little pile like that. Get a gallon of kerosene, pour it on top of the grass, set it on fire and burn it to the ground and the ashes will take root and grow.

"That ain't nothin'! You can go out to your 'tater patch or lettuce bed and clean it with a fine tooth comb. You can get the old woman's sifter and sift it until you know there ain't a sprig in there. Then you get your tweezers from your medicine cabinet and pick up every bit of it. Then you go out there and douse it with carbolic acid, so now you know you ain't got nary bit. You can go to sleep and tomorrow wake up and think 'no Bermuda grass!'

But the next day, let a little wind come and one sprig of it from your neighbor's field over there be blowed over to your field—just blowed over there and the shadow will take root and grow! Brother, I'm tellin' you right now, when you've got Bermuda grass, you've got it!"

After this humorous story, Evans continued, "You know, the gospel is like that. Once the gospel has come into the world, there's no power on heaven or earth or any other place that can destroy it. It's the gospel of the Kingdom and as long as there are people on the face of the earth and this world makes its orbit around the sun, the gospel will be proclaimed. Why? Because it is forever beginning. It's like being renewed. It's like an eternal spring. There's no way in the world to do away with the gospel once it has been planted on the earth by our Father because he is forever restoring his creation."

Notice how "Tex" was never content to hurry through a scene. He saw it so vividly that he wanted the hearer to visualize it as well. The one who preaches and testifies is responsible to help others see the truth of the gospel in order that they might respond to that truth.

Action

The witness is responsible for helping the hearer respond to the message. Unless a means of responding to the message is given, the message floats away with the breath of the one who utters it. In mainline churches the invitation has become the most neglected element in worship. We believe the moment is right to recover this crucial element in Christian worship. We have shown how some speakers have difficulty getting "off the ground." Larger numbers have even greater difficulty in landing.

Our esteemed colleague, the late O. Dean Martin, was forever asking the question, "What do you do after you preach?" He believed that those moments immediately following the sermon were of paramount significance. This conviction ran so deep in Dean Martin that he wrote one of the most helpful books ever written on the Christian invitation, *Invite: What to Do After the Sermon.* His book is filled with practical suggestions, and readers are strongly urged to secure his text as a companion volume to this present work. The "action" step is so vital in preaching and testifying that we shall devote the next chapter to it.

Part Four

Communicating
the
Gospel

Chapter Nine

Inviting
Response

I t must be acknowledged that every good thing in this world can be trivialized and misused and thus made to look futile and unimportant. There is no truth, idea, or method that is not abused by someone. And there is no denying that much has taken place in the name of preaching and testifying that has been of little significance and perhaps even deterred the kingdom of God. The invitation to Christian discipleship is an area of worship that has been so abused and neglected that it needs careful consideration. But, no matter how abused or neglected, abuse is never justification for abandonment.

The cautions and principles outlined in this chapter have grown out of our conviction that when the gospel is proclaimed, the invitation is imperative. We offer this instruction in the belief that when these cautions and principles are faithfully followed and when the proclaimer trusts fully in the Holy Spirit, a situation is created in which the possibility for divine-human encounter is greatly enhanced.

Let us remember that new life in Christ is a gift as well as a goal. Like all of God's gifts, this new life in Christ must be appropriated by a response of faith. Our part in this divine-human transaction might be described as bringing about occasions for people's response to Jesus Christ. How does one do this without putting obstacles in the path or getting in the way of God's work in people's lives? The following cautions and principles were born out of many years of struggle with this question. As a result of a long process of trial and error and trusting the Lord for direction, we offer the following learnings.

Cautions Needing Assessment

The following precautions are designed to facilitate our reflective process as we face this important and rather frightening responsibility. These are caution flags that are important to consider as we move into this exceedingly sensitive area.

1. *Preaching and testifying for a verdict can provoke hostility and resentment in some hearers.* We would be derelict if we did not mention this at the outset. Some people have been exploited and victimized by a brand of so-called evangelistic witnessing that has succeeded only in creating guilt and resentment. Some of us could supply illustrations of this point from our own personal pilgrimages. One of the most poignant illustrations was given by a pastor from Indiana:

> Another bad memory is of those earnest people who urged you to go to the altar during the invitation hymn. Then, they prayed and cried over you in the hope that God would rescue you from your evil ways. You were only eight or ten! You were not sure what they meant by evil ways.
>
> The sermon illustrations didn't apply to you. You had never been drunk—although you had, one time, tasted whiskey from a discarded bottle. You had never been out with another man's wife—although you did, one time, see a girl's petticoat when she was jumping rope. You had never gambled away your week's wages that would have put food on the table for your family—although you did, one time, play penny ante. You had never robbed a bank with a gun and been sent to prison—although you did sneak cookies from the jar.

As you knelt between your Sunday school teacher and your aunt and heard the preacher praying loudly, you felt sorry for all the women who were crying. It always made you feel a little embarrassed. But you didn't know what you had done that was so bad that they should be crying and begging God to save your poor, lost, miserable soul.

You look back on that experience (if you had such an experience) with mixed feelings. You appreciate the concern of those people of the past. With the exception of the altar call time, they did seem to understand you. But you resent the guilt feelings their efforts created in you. You resent having been dragged to the front. So you may resent the words "sin," "salvation," "Savior," "lay witness," "altar call," "evangelist," and "evangelism" without really knowing the roots of your resentment.

No matter how theologically appropriate the call for response or how sensitively we handle the matter, the moment we attempt to create an occasion for people to respond to the gospel is the moment that some people will infer "guilt by association." The fact that we are inviting response tends to identify us with those persons out of the past who were exploitative and demeaning. Therefore, we may become objects of their verbal abuse, or worse, they may decide to ignore us by boycotting worship services. Because these people have been wounded by others, we must treat them with the greatest patience and loving care.

2. *Preaching and testifying for response can degenerate into something negative and irresponsible.* In parts of the American church scene, the invitation is little more than an appeal to join the local church. It is an institutional appeal tacked on to the sermon. In many cases, the point of the sermon has nothing to do with the point of the invitation. Unfortunately, this reductionist approach serves to buttress the maintenance mentality and posture of the church—the idea that our responsibility is to maintain the institutional church at all costs and in every way. Many people probably have this idea confirmed when they attend church Sunday after Sunday and hear only two basic invitations: "Come attend the church" and "Come join the church."

Moreover, our invitation can degenerate into mere propositional or dogmatic religion. This is especially true when people hear invitations that insinuate: "If you believe these things, come and join!" There is a real danger in encouraging people to give mental ascent to a list of dogmatic propositions rather than discovering a living faith in the living God. There may be real danger in encouraging our people to repeat the Apostles' Creed too frequently and without reflecting on its meaning. Such a process suggests that if they believe the propositions of the creed, they *then* and *thereby* know Christ. A propositional religion is quite different from a living faith. We can believe things or ideas, but trust is reserved for persons. The object of Christian faith is not a list of doctrinal propositions but the living God revealed in Jesus of Nazareth whom we call the Christ.[1]

3. *Let us remember never to canonize a particular method.* There is a tendency to find only one way of giving an invitation and insist that all persons come through that mode. This form of "Xerox evangelism" betrays the biblical model. In the biblical narrative we find that there are countless ways by which persons are invited to faith and repentance. As we have seen in chapter seven, this variety is highlighted not only by a high level of sensitivity to particular persons and their needs, but also by various contexts. A form of invitation entirely appropriate for particular persons in one context may not be appropriate for persons in a radically different context.

4. *Let us remember that the purpose is not to put pressure on people but to alleviate it.* Leighton Ford tells about a high-pressure evangelist in the Wheaton College Chapel "whose finger swept the audience like an avenging angel; his invitation was so broad we felt we should come forward if we hadn't written our grandmother in the last week! He squeezed and pleaded as if Jesus were some kind of spiritual beggar rather than the royal Lord."[2]

Preachers and lay witnesses are involved in the process as a part of God's gracious concern for people. We are not required to convert anyone. That is God's business. If there is pressure in the encounter, and there may well be, it ought to be that of God's disclosure and not of our doing. As we have seen, people live constantly under the pressure of high-powered sales techniques. If we come across as another sales expert trying to get people to sign on the dotted line or purchase the product, then we have missed the mark. Our responsibility, rather, is to create an atmosphere or an occasion of freedom in which people can respond authentically to the leadership of the Holy Spirit. The moment we short-circuit people's freedom by using a high-pressured technique is the moment that we have overstepped our bounds as advocates of the gospel. An attitude of genuine respect for the response of the hearer must be conveyed. Anything short of this tends to violate human integrity.

It may, however, be a more destructive form of manipulation if a witness presents the message and does not allow a means of response. When we raise people's hopes and expectations or when the Holy Spirit convicts, it is imperative to give people an opportunity to respond. For us, it is as inconsistent to present the gospel without inviting a response, as it is to break the bread and lift the cup and not invite response.

5. *Let us remember that our fundamental purpose is not to separate but to unite, not to create chaos but koinonia.* The grace of God brings community, freedom, and unity—not schism and bondage. As the apostle Paul affirms, "God is a God not of disorder but of peace" (1 Cor. 14:33).

We, the authors, confess that we have not always known this! When we were younger in the faith, we felt it was our responsibility to present the gospel in such a way that we separated the sheep from the goats, the wheat from the tares. Now that we are older we see the folly of this. First, God has never given over to any of us the prerogative of separating the sheep from the goats. Second, there is so much "goat" in all of us that we would not know where to begin! In preaching for a response, our purpose is not to separate but to unite.

6. *We must caution ourselves to always be honest, clear, and non-exploitative.* It is not altogether honest to say, "We will sing three verses of a hymn" and then proceed to sing eleven verses. In the minds of some this impugns the integrity of the communicator. Moreover, we must be very careful in the use of standard invitations that tend to be exploitative. For instance, many of us have seen this form of invitation: The congregation is asked to stand for the singing of one verse of a hymn. Afterward, the preacher says, "If you were to die at midnight tonight, where would your soul spend eternity? Do you have the deep abiding assurance that you would go to heaven? Does God's spirit bear record with your spirit that you are a child of God? If you have that deep assurance in your heart, would you please be seated at this time and be very much in prayer for those persons who cannot witness to such an assurance." Next, the preacher instructs that every head should be bowed and every eye closed. Then he says to those standing, "If you would like the church to remember you in prayer, if you know in your heart that you are not right with God, if you would like for me to remember you in my prayers, would you please raise your hand."

One preacher went so far as to insist that a large clock with three hands be put on the back wall of the sanctuary. This gave him the freedom to say immediately, "Yes, I see that hand, I see that hand, I see that hand!" (One response for the hour hand, one for the minute hand, and one for the second hand!) After saying, "Yes, I see that hand" three times, this preacher insisted that the meek would begin to raise their hands. This is a vile form of exploitation. It assumes that in order to seduce the goose you must have the proper gander! Every communicator of the gospel would do well to heed the admonition of Dr. Raymond Bailey: "Seduction was the way of the serpent, not the way of Christ. . . . Surely our task is to present the gospel in the clearest terms in order to allow the listeners to make a free and intelligent choice. The truth of God should not require subterfuge. I cannot think of a single biblical narrative that records God's entrapment of a convert. Deceit is not a divine technique."[3]

Principles That Give Integrity

Just as there are cautions that need to be assessed in inviting response, so there are principles that give integrity to one's attempt to extend the invitation. When we say *principles* we are not insinuating that these are hard and fast rules that must be followed in every situation. These are not laws chiseled in granite but principles that give guidance. These principles have been hammered out on the anvil of our own experience, and we dare to believe that they are trustworthy. However, we are always open to new learnings through the inspiration of the Holy Spirit working in our own lives and through the lives of those sisters and brothers from whom we have learned so much.

1. Personal-Relational Invitations

Christian invitations are given and responded to from within the context of the Christian community. This is true even with regard to one-to-one witness. In the one-to-one encounter, the person giving the testimony and invitation is always a representative person. The person who bears witness does so as a part of the community of faith, the Body of Christ. Therefore, the invitation extended is not his or her invitation. That is to say, the invitation is not the property of

the one who extends it. The invitation is given on behalf of
Christ and the community of faith.

Moreover, the one who hears the witness and responds to
the invitation never does so in isolation. Even persons who
have come to faith in Christ in prison cells have done so as a
result of the prevenient grace of God working through the
witness of some brother or sister, and most often, a series of
brothers and sisters. It seems that God never enters into a
personal relationship with someone apart from other persons.

Here we see the importance of the congregation. It is God's
will that the people of God be drawn together in
congregational support. From beginning to end, the Bible is
concerned with God's purpose in seeking, inviting, and
creating a people. Peter summarized a quote from Exodus
19:5-6 when he declared, "But you are a chosen race, a royal
priesthood, a holy nation, God's own people, in order that
you may proclaim the mighty acts of him who called you out of
darkness into his marvelous light" (1 Pet. 2:9). The fact that
God's inviting and seeking love reaches out to us through the
history of the men and women of the Old Testament and
ultimately through the person of Jesus Christ is ample
evidence that God speaks to persons through persons. This
not only affirms the personal-relational nature of God it also
teaches us that people are never "born again" in isolation. It is
impossible for us to exist as Christians apart from this world of
the personal and relational. Even when we are "born again"
we are being born into a family. This truth gives great
encouragement both to the person doing the inviting and also
to the person being invited.

Dr. Maxie Dunnam gives a poignant illustration of this
truth. He cites a reference from Truman Capote's book
Other Voices, Other Rooms. The hero is about to walk along
a heavy but rotting beam over a brooding, murky creek.
Starting over, "stepping gingerly . . . he felt he would never
reach the other side: Always he would be balanced here,

suspended between land and in the dark and alone. Then feeling the board shake as Idabel started across, he remembered that he had someone to be together with. And he could go on."

Dunnam asks, "Isn't this our experience?" And he replies, "It certainly has been mine. I shiver at the thought of having to go it alone. I get chills when I consider where I might be if at the right time I had not felt the board shake because someone was walking with me!" He goes on to say, "The Christian walk is a shared journey. We do not walk alone; others walk with us."[4] This is the experience of each person who gives the invitation and each who responds. When an invitation is extended, the invitation is experienced in the context of the Christian community. When an invitation is given it may come through a solo voice, but it is always backed up by a chorus of "amens" and "hallelujahs" sung by a loving community of faith. The response may occur with one person, but it takes place in the midst of "a cloud of witnesses" (Heb. 12:1). When a person responds, all of the people are affected. Jesus said that there is even rejoicing "in heaven over one sinner who repents" (Luke 15:7).

2. Invitation Flows from the Message

The Christian invitation is an extension of the very nature of the gospel. The invitation is not something that is tacked on to the end of the testimony or sermon as if it were an appendage. To the contrary, it is a vital part of the gospel. As previously stated, God is seeking to reveal God's self through the message. Thus, it is the self-disclosing God who is doing the inviting. Our responsibility is to participate in this occasion and try not to put any obstacles in the path of this divine-human encounter.

The invitation and the content of the witness are organically linked, but the invitation is always secondary to the message. In other words, the invitation grows out of the message and not the reverse. This means that the message is normative. It also means that the parameters of the invitation are set by the parameters of the message. That is, the shape of the invitation is determined by the shape of the message. The content of the message sets the content of the invitation. The two are organically linked, but one's understanding of the order of *authority* is critical. Therefore, in order to lend clarity, the witness must be able to state the purpose of the message in a simple declarative sentence.

The purpose of the message is not the theme or thesis of the message but the response that is being sought. If the invitation is an extension of the message, the point of the message must be clear if the point of the invitation is to be clear. Since the two are organically linked and congruent, each depends upon the other for meaning and clarity.

While vacationing in a western state we worshiped with a congregation in a rural area where agriculture was the primary industry. The majority of the people in the congregation were, in some ways, connected with farming. We happened to be there on "Rogation Sunday." This is a day of thanksgiving and prayer that focuses on the harvest and proper stewardship of God's good creation. The young pastor chose a text from the creation story in Genesis and did an outstanding job of exegeting the passage and interpreting for his people the Judeo-Christian understanding of stewardship of the soil. We were all impressed by the message, but it was obvious that the farmers and their families were profoundly moved. When the young man finished his message there was a "holy hush" in the sanctuary. One could feel the urge from within the people to respond to the clear call growing out of the message. However, we were appalled when the pastor gave an invitation for people to join the church either on transfer of letter or profession of faith. There was no response to this invitation, but one could feel the deep restlessness and disappointment of the congregation. What was the problem?

The point of the invitation was not in keeping with the point of the message. The method of invitation was not congruent with the purpose of the sermon. Instead of the invitation growing out of the message, the invitation was a "tack on."

Not only does the content of the message set the content of the invitation, but also, the shape of the message sets the shape of the invitation. The meaning and method of the invitation must be congruent with the message itself. Otherwise, people are apt to become confused and frustrated.

3. A Response of Faith

When structuring an invitation for response, the witness must make sure that the invitation includes options, and the witness must respect all responses. The witness should never say, "If you do not respond at this moment, you may never have another opportunity!" This is pure rubbish! It is a scare technique to get people to respond out of fear. It is limiting options that we have no right to limit. Moreover, if an authentic "no" is registered or an authentic "perhaps" expressed, they deserve the same amount of respect as an authentic "yes."

Those of us who stand in the Armenian-Wesleyan tradition believe that human beings have been created in the image of God and are authentically free. This God-given freedom is so real that one can actually say "no" to the living God. This being the case, whatever form of invitation we offer must respect the sacred right of rejection. A good measuring device to authenticate methods of invitation is to ask: "Does the method preserve the freedom and authenticity of decision?" In preaching and testifying, our goal is always to seek a response of faith. Of course, we want that response to be favorable. But, just as we will risk refusal rather than betray the gospel, so will we prefer a negative decision to the shallowness of engineered consent. So often the outcome realized in manipulative methods is the securing of a conditioned response by triggering a hidden psychological need or personality deficiency over which the hearer cannot or does not exercise conscious control. This abuse of Christian communication does not result in solving a problem but in exploiting it.

Therefore, our concern is not to manipulate motives in order to achieve some desired result. Rather, we hope to bring the gospel to bear upon human beings in such a way that motives are purified so that a person can seek first the kingdom of God. We are not trying to get people to do the right thing for the wrong reason, but, insofar as possible, the right thing for the right reason. Methods of manipulation are usually geared to reduce the amount of the witness's risk of failure. They, therefore, violate the structure of decision and destroy people by depriving them of their God-given freedom.

There is a delicate line beyond which our attempts to convincingly witness the gospel become a license to exploit. When, instead of being used to encourage choice, persuasive testimony is used to subvert it, then our attempt at witnessing has become manipulative. Always, the best remedy for exploitative methodology is to offer Christ in all his fullness and winsomeness, and then let our lives and our words speak his challenge so clearly that people find the freedom to make their own decisions.

4. Commitment Is to God

The fourth principle highlights the need to always remember that the commitment is to the God of the disclosure and not to the gospel advocate. As we have seen earlier, precious human beings are never vital statistics. Therefore, people who respond positively are never, "feathers in our cap" or "jewels in our crown."

Again, we must remind the reader that this is not a negative bias against statistical data-gathering. We are always allowed to count as long as we do so in terms of the biblical perspective. Commenting on the growth of the early church, Luke says, "And day by day the Lord added to their number those whom he was saving" (Acts 2:47 NEB). This scripture clearly states that God does the saving, and it is God who adds people to the church. People were never intended to be our converts any more than they are intended to be our clones.

5. *Following the Incarnational Principle*

Our demeanor must reflect our firm conviction regarding the Incarnation. We do not present ourselves as saints calling poor miserable sinners to repent. To the contrary, as D. T. Niles said, we are more like "beggars telling other beggars where they can find bread." Preaching or testifying for response requires that we follow the incarnational principle of identification. This requires a self-emptying (see Philippians 2) of anything that would separate the witness from the people. Any expression of superiority by which the witness condescends in relating to people is a denial of the Incarnation. Christian witnessing goes astray if it is done in the spirit of pity for the heathen. Our belief in the Incarnation insists that the witness must engage in the pain, problems, pressures, and the fears, foibles, and frustrations of the human family. This is quite different than approaching people "from above." It is our calling to enter into the sufferings of people and allow ourselves to become vulnerable. We are like wounded healers. We know what it is like to suffer the pains of death and bondage of sin. Therefore, we stand alongside our brothers and sisters, offering the good news of the gospel and inviting response.

6. *Trusting the Holy Spirit*

Finally, the witness must trust the Holy Spirit. A person's response to God's disclosure is always a mystery. It is impossible to engineer the mysterious working of the Holy Spirit. The "wind [spirit] blows where it chooses" (John 3:8). In the final analysis, all the witness can do is love compassionately, attempt to relate to people in such a way that develops trust, present the gospel, and show how that gospel has intersected with one's own life. Hopefully persons, enabled by the power of the Holy Spirit, will respond to God's act of forgiveness in Jesus Christ. We sow the seeds of the gospel in anticipation of the harvest, but we cannot cause the harvest any more than the farmer can control the sun and the rain.

The miracle is that the Holy Spirit works through our weak and insufficient attempts. We always stand in awe of this profound truth. Often, when we have felt that we have said and done it all wrong, the Holy Spirit moves in the hearts and lives of persons and they respond in faith. This is a profound mystery, and it proves that the grace of God is greater than our semantics and goes beyond our blundering methodology. This is no excuse for poor semantics or blundering methodology, but it does accent the powerful grace of God working through ordinary human beings.

But, how do we create occasions for persons to respond to the living God? Are there methods of inviting response that respect the cautions and principles outlined in this chapter? In chapter 10 we will offer a wide array of practical methods.

Chapter Ten

Methods of Inviting Response

L et us assume that we have a clear grasp of the gospel so that we can verbalize it faithfully. Let us assume that we have developed a keen sensitivity to human need and a discernment regarding various contexts. Let us assume that we have prayerfully assessed the applicable cautions and principles involved in inviting response. What then? This question raises the immediate need for practical methods of invitation.

The purpose of the invitation is to make Christ's claims very clear and then to call our auditors to inquiry, repentance, and faith. The invitation can be offered in numerous ways, depending on the message, the awareness of need, the setting, and the leadership of the Holy Spirit. In this chapter we wish to offer a variety of ways of inviting response. We do not expect the reader to feel comfortable with all of the methods offered. We do hope that interest will be incited and those who preach and testify will be stimulated to develop creative approaches that are commensurate with the message of the gospel, the nature of the context, the personality and style of the one who witnesses and utilizes as many senses as possible.

Some methods are more appropriate for Sunday worship services conducted by ordained clergy. Some are more fitting for use by lay witnesses who have responsibility for occasional services. Others are suited for open-air services or settings beyond the local church, while others are more appropriate for one-to-one witness. Whatever the occasion for witness, we are assuming there is never a gospel presentation that is not invitational and does not call for response.

Just as there is no "canned" or single way of presenting the gospel, there is no "packaged" invitation appropriate for every occasion. Here we will present a wide variety of methods being used by Christians in various settings in many parts of the world. It is for each Christian witness to discover his or her mode of operation which fits his or her own style of preaching or testifying.[5]

Settings Beyond the Local Church

Alan Walker, former Director of World Evangelism for the World Methodist Council, has been a harbinger of invitational proclamation. The following method can be used in local church settings although it works best in mass meetings held in the open air, secular halls, theaters, etc.

At the close of his address Walker requests a period of silent prayer during which he invites people to surrender to Jesus Christ and to say in their hearts, "I commit my life to Jesus Christ in the fellowship of His Church." At the end of this period of silence he offers a prayer thanking God for those who have committed their lives to Christ and commends them to God's loving care. Then, he announces a hymn which expresses commitment and which has several eight-line verses. As the audience sings the first verse, Walker has instructed several pastors to come forward and stand facing the congregation with commitment cards in their hands. At the close of the first verse, he stops the singing and gives an open invitation to confess Christ. People are asked to come forward as the rest of the hymn is sung, take a card, and remain facing the pastors until the end of the meeting. At this point, he explains that there will be other trained counselors who will be coming forward during each remaining verse of the hymn. He explains that these counselors will not be receiving cards but will be there to stand with those who respond, to assist in signing the cards, offer a word of counsel and a prayer with each person. After the second verse of the hymn he again stops the singing and makes a further invitation. Another group of counselors walks forward along with those responding as the next verse is being sung. Before the fourth and last verse he makes a third appeal. At the end of this process, Walker speaks a few words of group counseling, voices a prayer, and explains that after the benediction, all who came forward, with their counselors, will move to a side room. Before the benediction he makes one further invitation. "After the benediction," he says, "I will join the pastors and offer cards of commitment, remaining until the hall is empty. The choir will re-sing that last hymn again as you leave. Please do not stay to listen, but as you go, remember we are still waiting. You may prefer to come forward now before you go home and we will welcome you. You may have the chance now to speak to someone with you—husband, wife, or friend, and you may wish to come together. If God has spoken to you tonight, come." Ordinarily, the commitment card contains two challenges: 1. I commit myself to Jesus Christ in the fellowship of His Church, and 2. I recommit myself to Jesus Christ for fuller service and witness. There is a place on the card for the signature, the date, and the church preference.[6]

We now know that John Wesley used various methods of extending the invitation that were appropriate to open-air witnessing or "field preaching." A manuscript written by one of Wesley's lay preachers describes how Wesley called people to commitment. Wesley would place his preachers and class leaders at the front of the crowd in order to help people who came forward under spiritual conviction. He would also scatter his helpers throughout the crowd in order to deal with those who showed signs of being moved by the power of the Holy Spirit.

Moreover, from time to time, Wesley held "after meetings." In the New Room located at Bristol, England, there is a little place to which people, who where "awakened" under Wesley's preaching, were invited to go for counseling and prayer. He used these methods as means of guiding people into his class and band meetings where they were nurtured and encouraged to journey on to holiness. It is interesting to note how variations of this basic method are still being used by those who take the courage to preach and to testify in settings beyond the local church.[7]

When preaching and testifying beyond local church settings, it is necessary to offer people opportunities for inquiry. Some people are dealing with intellectual problems and questions. They may not know enough to respond to a challenge to commit their lives. These persons need to be invited to *inquire,* and we need to provide occasions and classes for inquiry. These classes can be dialogue times focused on intellectual wrestling with Christian faith. The authors have found it helpful to advertise these "inquirer's classes" in the secular press. Persons who respond are making only one commitment: To inquire or ask hard questions regarding the Christian faith.

Toward the end of his life, Harry Denman, a layman and former General Secretary of the Methodist General Board of Evangelism, recommended the use of *question and answer* settings. He advocated this technique not only for the sake of "outsiders" who wish to inquire regarding the Christian faith but as an effective method for deepening the spiritual life of members. He contended that people know their needs and they need an arena where they can express those needs freely. Denman believed that this would give the one who preaches or testifies an opportunity to say a lot of things in the form of testimony while responding directly to the real questions of real people.

Joe Hale, General Secretary of the World Methodist

Council, gives an outstanding illustration of how the Inquiry Room can be used effectively in settings beyond the local church.

An Inquiry Room near the place of worship may be arranged with forty or fifty chairs in place. During the closing hymn, persons are invited to remain for a brief after-session to receive further instruction regarding the theme of the sermon or testimony. If the theme has been on "the assurance of faith" then the after-session can offer brief instruction on the subject, "steps to Christian assurance." The people are asked to make their way to the Inquiry Room while the final hymn is being sung. The leader says, "What you are saying if you make this response is simply this: 'I want to hear more about the subject of the evening and I would like to join you for this session, in which you share some ideas that will help me grasp more significantly the meaning of assurance.'" The people are not asked to come to the front of the meeting place but to go directly to a prearranged room while the final hymn is being sung. On the concluding verse the leader joins those who have responded, and leaves the service in charge of someone else who makes closing remarks and pronounces the benediction.

Hale believes that the after-session itself should be conducted in a conversational manner. He says:

When the people have gathered I thank the people for wanting to remain for this short period and simply share informally, as I would speak with one individual, how to find Christian assurance. . . . Sometimes I feel it appropriate to offer prayer, sentence by sentence, in which those who desire may share. Sometimes it seems appropriate to give the people the chance to record on a three-by-five card their own understandings of what it means to be a Christian. I do not ask these persons to sign the cards unless they want to do so. If they feel they are pressured to write something and put their name to it, they feel "trapped" because no mention of this was made in the invitation. Afterwards, Hale says that he stands at the door of the room and speaks to the people as they leave, thus making himself available for further counseling.

Reiner Dauner, Regional Secretary of Evangelism for the Methodist Church of Germany, outlines another method which creates an occasion for people to make a first time commitment to Christ. He says:

> During my closing prayer I ask the people to bow and be in a spirit of prayer. Then, I ask those who wish to make a decision for Christ to lift their hands. I find that people are freer to do this if they do not feel they are being watched by others. Afterwards, I pray a "decision prayer" and invite those who wish to do so to make their own decision by repeating the prayer after me sentence-by-sentence. Sometimes I distribute a card with a decision prayer already printed on it and invite the people to pray it together aloud. After this time of prayer, I call the people to come forward and light a little candle from a large candle which symbolizes Jesus "the light of the world." Finally, in Germany we have in our Methodist churches, a card on which is printed: "I have chosen Jesus Christ as my Savior and King and I desire to follow Him. I ask Him to take control of my life and I want to be His servant forever." I offer this card to the people while greeting them at the exit. The people are encouraged to sign the card and write the date and the place on it. This becomes a very important remembrance of a transforming commitment.

Methods Appropriate for the Sanctuary

Some methods of invitation are better suited for use during regular worship services in local churches. Invitations are greatly needed in our churches. Inside many congregations there are sincere persons who are on the fringe of faith. They have no certainty of Christian faith or no fulfilling personal relationship with Jesus Christ. The church seldom deals, at any level of seriousness, with the possibility of persons in the

congregation who are still unconverted. There are those who
tend to fall into the view that everyone who is baptized is
converted. However, any sensible observer will notice very
quickly how much uncertainty, resident agnosticism and
works righteousness there is in almost every congregation. As
is pointed out in the letters to the seven churches in
Revelation, it is possible for a congregation to start out well
and then slowly but surely get off on an alien agenda, forget
why it is called, whom it is called to serve, and the One who
has called it into being (Rev. 2–3). Thus, congregations that
consist of good, respectable people who are well organized
with all the appropriate committees, sometimes haven't the
foggiest notion regarding either their identity or their
vocation. Therefore, the need is critical for preaching and
testifying for a verdict and calling for a response as a regular
agenda item in local congregations. The so-called "nominal or
notional Christian" may be listed in the church membership,
but they are a far cry from the repentance and faith required
for conversion and the holy life of discipleship which is an
outgrowth of sanctification.

There is nothing contradictory about preaching and
testifying for a verdict and offering an invitation to Christian
discipleship "inside the church." This is simply a part of our
responsibility to keep the excitement, promises, and
demands of the gospel of Jesus Christ always before the
congregation. This must be done on a week-to-week basis.

The late O. Dean Martin's book addresses the challenge of
offering an invitation for response on a week-to-week basis in
the local church. His book is written for pastors, but it is
recommended reading for all lay witnesses as well. Martin
outlines an example of decisive invitation which he used at
the end of nearly every sermon he preached. He says:

> At the close of the service I ask the congregation to bow their
> heads and make their pew an altar of prayer. I ask them to

consider prayerfully the key idea of the message of the service, which might be conversion, social responsibility, stewardship, or being more loving. I then give them adequate time on their own to deal with the subject as they can and if they will, during private, individual prayer. On many occasions, for those who want to respond but do not know "the right words," I slowly word a prayer that might assist them in making a meaningful commitment concerning this subject.

I make a strong effort to place myself in the same frame of mind as if I were kneeling at the altar rail with an individual and he/she was saying, "Pastor, I want to act on this proposition but I don't know how to pray." In a personalized case like that, I would help the individual word an appropriate prayer. And, I have learned that most of our people do not know how to pray specifically concerning specific personal needs. I therefore respond to their earnest quest. . . . I also often add, "If you are here and do not have the courage to respond to this message, or are simply not ready, or are just not interested, then you are invited to remain courteous and patient. No one is going to manipulate you here. The service will be dismissed shortly." This simple and occasional addition to our "group counseling" time can convey many meaningful things to people throughout the congregation.[8]

The Response Guide

Dr. Lawrence Lacour, one of the original architects of the New Life Mission movement, developed a method of invitation using *Response Guides*. This method was later refined by Dr. George Gill Hunter, III, Dean of the E. Stanley Jones School for World Mission, and has proven to be a highly effective way of enabling people to make commitments in terms of five different categories for response. These categories are: One's relationship to God, the church, other people, the world, and the self. A number of possible commitments are listed under each category. A model to aid in the preparation of a response guide can be found in the Appendix. The model is merely a suggestion and each gospel advocate is encouraged to fashion the response guide in terms of the specific needs of local situations and in terms of specific themes addressed in sermon or testimony. Some witnesses or missioners use the entire form each evening with multiple challenges listed under each of the five basic categories. Others feel that it is better to use a shorter version of the response guide and focus attention upon very specific challenges. At any rate, it is better to "tailor" the response guide to fit definite objectives and themes.

Most response guides are printed on bulletin size mimeograph sheets. On one side of the folded sheet there appears a clear rationale for calling for response to the gospel. On the other side the four categories of response are listed along with particular challenges within each category. Some gospel advocates use the response guide at the close of each worship service during a protracted mission. Others choose to use the response guide only at the final service in a series of services. The response guides should be handed out to every person who enters for worship.

Ordinarily, the response guide is used in the following manner:

> After the sermon or testimony, invite persons to bow for a moment of silent prayer. Encourage the people to ask God what response/responses God calls them to make or to make known. Following the prayer, the witness proceeds somewhat as follows: "Tonight as you entered for worship you received a response guide entitled 'Why Call For A Decision?' It is my prayer that this response guide will become more than simply a sheet of paper upon which we put a series of check marks. Rather, I pray that these pieces of paper will become symbols of our lives. In a few moments these responses will be received and placed on the altar of the church as we all bow together for a closing prayer. Obviously, these response guides are not your covenant with God, but they are a record of that covenant.

Therefore, I ask that each of us take a pencil and, as an interpretation is given of each response, let us make those commitments we feel God would have us make."

After this brief introductory statement, it is helpful to encourage the people to read both the rationale for the Christian invitation and the various challenges that are listed. This can be accomplished by calling for a brief time of silent meditation. Then, it is helpful to interpret each of the responses, sentence by sentence, explaining what is meant by each challenge. At each point the people are invited to indicate their responses. Following this period of spiritual inventory the people are requested to pass the response guides to the center aisles. These are gathered by the ushers and brought forward. The leaders then add their own response sheets to those which have been collected and take all to the altar. The congregation is then asked to stand while the leader prays a prayer of commitment and dedication. At times it is helpful to encourage those who wish to do so to gather around the altar for the dedicatory prayer. This is especially meaningful in churches with an architectural design that allows the people to gather around the table of the Lord.

Writing Your Own Prayer

Many who preach and testify have found the use of small cards a most helpful means in enabling persons to respond to the gospel. These cards can be made available in the pew racks or they can be passed out at the door as the people enter. This method of invitation goes by several names (written response, writing your most earnest prayer, writing your most heartfelt prayer) but the mode of operation seems to be similar in each case.

After the sermon or testimony the witness calls for a time of silent prayer in which the people are encouraged to write their deepest, most heartfelt prayer. This is an especially helpful experience for lay persons. Though pastors are accustomed to the discipline of writing prayers, many lay persons have never attempted to write a prayer. Once the people have written their prayers several options are available. During the closing hymn the prayer cards can be received by the ushers, brought to the altar of the church, and presented with a prayer of dedication. Some leaders prefer to have the people bring their written prayers forward, kneel for a few moments at the kneeling rail and leave the prayers "face down" inside the kneeling rail. Others prefer to encourage the people to take the written prayers home with them as a remembrance of a time of commitment and worship. It is possible to offer a combination of these options, and to indicate the nature of these options before the prayers are written.

There is some general consensus that this method of invitation may have gotten its start in a church in Pennsylvania. Early in the 1960's a New Life Mission was conducted in this church. One month before the mission was to begin, the missioner received a distressing phone call from the local pastor. Several members of the "official board" of his church had been involved in sexual indiscretions with one another. One of the women involved had made a public confession—naming names! Therefore, all of the sordid details became "community property." As a result, the church was torn asunder. The pastor asked the missioner if it would be possible for him to preach a sermon on the "Christian View of Sex." The pastor needed an answer right away as he wished to advertise the theme of the message in the local press. The missioner agreed but suggested that the title ought to be "The Judeo-Christian View of Human Sexuality." Miraculously, on that particular evening the sanctuary was filled to capacity. In preparation, the pastor and the missioner had thought and prayed regarding the form that the invitation should take. It was the local pastor who suggested the method of writing prayers on three-by-five cards. After the quiet time the people were encouraged to bring their prayers forward, kneel for a few moments at the kneeling rail and place their prayers face down inside the rail. The missioner kept one of the cards left at the altar. It reads: "Lord give me the strength and the power to leave her alone and stay with my wife. Lord, I have sinned against you, my wife and my family. Lord, I have brought reproach upon your church. Please forgive me, I am so weak, but in your strength and power I know that I can do the right thing. Lord, have mercy on me and forgive me. In Jesus' name. Amen."

The Prayer Time

Another effective method of invitation is sometimes referred to as the "prayer time" or the "quiet time." Generally, this method involves inviting the people to approach the altar or kneeling rail for a time of prayer at the close of the service and return to their seats when they are ready to do so. This method can be used during evening services in a special mission or it is a very effective form of invitation for the regular Sunday morning worship service.

If employed during a protracted mission, the method usually takes this form:

> It is necessary to make arrangements with the ushers so that at the conclusion of the service the lights in the sanctuary are lowered in order to highlight or focus attention upon the altar. At the time of the announcements the leader should alert the people as to how the service will close. The leader's statement might include: "Following my message I want to give each of you the opportunity to kneel at the altar of this church—much as we do when we receive holy communion, except tonight you will come at the time you choose and stay for as little or as long as you desire. We will not partake of the element of holy communion. I have asked our musicians to play several familiar hymns of invitation. During the playing of these hymns, come and offer your prayer. When you have finished, you may be on

your way. You may want to pray for some special need in your own life, for forgiveness, for your concern as a Christian for the world, or offer a prayer of thanksgiving for God's presence with us. At the close of my address I will ask as many of you as will to join the pastor and myself as we offer our prayers at the kneeling rail. As soon as there is a vacancy here at the kneeling rail by one leaving, another will come immediately and take that place. Some of you may be saying, 'Can't I pray here where I am sitting?' Of course, the answer is 'yes.' If you would feel more comfortable offering your prayer in the pew, please do so, but I would encourage you to offer a very definite prayer focused upon very definite needs in your life. There will be no formal benediction to this service. When we have finished our prayers we will consider the service dismissed and quietly be on our way." The leader states, "We now invite you to commune with God."

It is important to give an option to people who may be visiting or who may not want to kneel at the kneeling rail. At the close of the sermon or testimony, this invitation should be reiterated for the sake of clarity. (See Joe Hale, *Design for Evangelism,* for a more complete explanation of this method).

The authors often use this method and add the following variation. For the first night of the mission, the method is followed as listed above. Thereafter, the following procedure is added:

We announce to the people that after we have joined with them in prayer at the kneeling rail we (along with the pastor) will come inside the kneeling rail and make ourselves available for special prayer requests. If the people have a special prayer request to make, we encourage them to raise their hand while kneeling at the rail. Whereupon, we kneel before them and ask, "May I help you?" Upon hearing the request, we often lay on hands and pray very specifically with that particular person in terms of his or her particular request. This gives both the local pastor and the witness the opportunity to minister with the people.

The "prayer time" method is also appropriate for the regular Sunday morning worship service. While serving as parish ministers, both authors employed the method. Working closely with our worship committees we devised a plan to enable our people to creatively use the kneeling rail in the sanctuary. We secured permission to include in the order of worship the following copy beneath the "Invitation to Christian Discipleship."

> The kneeling rail in (United) Methodist churches has been traditionally a place of prayer. If you have cause for thanksgiving, desire forgiveness, have a special need or desire to pray where countless others have prayed before you, you are invited to join the pastors at the kneeling rail for your private prayer during the singing of this hymn. You may remain for a moment or for the entire singing of the hymn.

The people are invited to come and go in much the same way as listed above. It is helpful to encourage the choir to be ready to sing the hymn over. There may be those who are waiting to kneel and pray and have not had the opportunity to do so.

After employing this method for two or three months we noticed that the people were overcoming their fear of the kneeling rail. Thus, we asked our worship committees for permission to make ourselves available for individual prayer requests. Following our own prayers with the people at the kneeling rail, we would go inside the rail and respond to those people who raised their hands indicating a need for special prayer. This enabled us, on a week-to-week basis, to pray with our people during the regular Sunday morning worship service. Our willingness to make ourselves available to our people during these times also signaled our willingness to be available for times of private counsel. Therefore, on numerous occasions, we found opportunities to invite the people who raised their hands at the rail to meet us for private counsel during the following week. In addition, on a regular basis we invited persons to make a public declaration of their faith by coming forward during the singing of the final hymn.

An Invitation to Healing

Roy Johansen, Regional Secretary for World Evangelism in Northern Europe, has discovered an immense hunger for healing on the part of people. He believes that people not only desire healing for the body but for the mind, spirit, and human relationships as well. To respond to this need, Johansen utilizes the following method:

> After the sermon or testimony, I call for a period of silence so that my message can be absorbed and the Holy Spirit can do His work. Then I pray, "Jesus, I am your servant and I have just preached your Gospel. Now, I expect that you will confirm the message in people's hearts, and I look forward to seeing your miracle working hand extended toward all of us. Amen." Then I say, "If you believe what I have told you is true, why not accept it? You cannot neglect the challenge. You need to open your life to Christ, make your decision for Him and receive your miracle for your life." After this challenge I ask, "If you have something in your life you believe Jesus can heal, if you need a miracle of body, mind, soul, spirit, or a healing miracle for your relationships, please lift your hand." Then, I invite the people to stand for the singing of a hymn while those who wish to do so, are invited to come forward for prayer. For those who come forward I say, "This gives us an opportunity to pray for one another."

Many, through the ministry of this devoted pastor-evangelist, are discovering that Jesus Christ truly does offer healing for the whole person.

Sacramental Invitations

It is obvious to anyone who has read the ritual for Holy Communion that "invitation" is an inseparable part of both "Word and Table." The liturgy for the Lord's Supper not only

contains a powerful declaration of the gospel, it also contains a
powerful call for repentance and faith. For a number of years
the authors have worked with a method that ties response to
Christ directly with the Eucharist. Following the sermon the
pastor says:

> All along in this mission our attempt has been to create
> occasions that would allow the Holy Spirit to work in our midst
> and bring new life to His church. We have sought this new life
> in terms of the renewal of the faith and life of the church and
> the recovery of the mission of the church in the world. Now we
> come to the final evening in this series. Probably, the Holy
> Spirit has been speaking to you all along. It would be relatively
> easy for all of us to respond to the convicting power of the Holy
> Spirit by simply resolving "to do better." It is helpful to make a
> commitment that is more concrete; a commitment in which the
> content is spelled out. Surely, many of you have already felt
> the deep need to enter into a new covenant with God that can
> be expressed in your daily life.
>
> Therefore, I would like to issue the following invitation: If
> you have decided to accept Jesus Christ and you wish to pledge
> your allegiance to his Kingdom, after the benediction for this
> service I invite you to step into the prayer chapel. Or, if you
> have looked at your life through the power of the Holy Spirit,
> and now you realize the desperate need to renew your
> dedication to Jesus Christ and to reaffirm your vows, then I
> invite you to move into the prayer chapel immediately
> following the benediction. Please enter the chapel quietly and
> be seated for a few moments of silent prayer and meditation. In
> the prayer chapel we will enter into a new covenant with God
> and then partake of Holy Communion in order to seal the
> covenant we are making. We are doing this because we feel the
> invitation to Holy Communion is the most searching invitation
> to new life which can be offered.

In preparation for this special communion service, we have
sometimes found it helpful to combine parts of the ritual of
the John Wesley Covenant Service with the ritual for Holy

Communion. A careful reading of both rituals will show the reader how this can be done. Since in our tradition, Holy Communion is served only by ordained clergy, if the witness is a lay person it is necessary to work very carefully with the local pastor in the preparation for this very special opportunity for response.

In the Methodist churches of West Africa tremendous emphasis is given to the New Year's Eve Watch Night Service. On these occasions great crowds gather very early for worship. Using the full ritual for John Wesley's Covenant Service, the people are invited to renew their vows. The service becomes a dramatic form of invitation. About five minutes before midnight all of the lights are turned off in the sanctuary and the leader announces that the old year, with all of its sins and burdens, is passing into history and a new year, a new beginning is about to dawn. At exactly twelve midnight the enormous Christ candle on the altar lights up the darkness. Light, taken from the Christ candle, is spread throughout the sanctuary until there is light everywhere. There is great rejoicing and dancing before God as a renewed people face a new year with new challenges and opportunities.

We have mentioned only a limited number of practical methods or rituals. There are many more that are being employed by those who preach and testify. Some methods are appropriate only for specific situations. Others seem to have a broader usefulness. We challenge the reader to follow the leadership of the Holy Spirit in creating new ways to invite response with integrity.

Chapter Eleven

Taking the Stand

I n chapter eight, we gave instruction regarding the organization of the message in terms of communication theory. We believe that careful attention must be given to the way the message is structured. Equally important is the manner of delivery. How shall we present the message? The demeanor of the witness is a critical element in the credibility of the testimony. Often in a court of law, it is the body language of the witness that makes him or her believable.

As stated previously, the message is the message. Each witness must be faithful to his or her own being and personality. But the very manner in which we preach and testify greatly impacts the way the message is perceived and heard. So often those who preach and testify spend very little time in preparation for the delivery of the message. Again, it is important that one hears the admonition; delivery is a vital part of the total message. The witness in his or her style must be faithful to the Creator, but this is no excuse for being dull!

Importance of Nonverbal Communication

A most effective communicator of the gospel, Dr. Joe Harding, reminds us of the importance of nonverbal factors in communications. In reality only seven percent of communication is verbal. Thirty-eight percent of the content is conveyed by tone of voice and fifty-five percent is through body language. The tendency is to focus all of our time and energy on only seven percent of the total experience of preaching and testifying. Harding says we often miss the tones and feeling of the written message of scripture. He advises one to endeavor to get inside the experience or the story in the Bible. Walk around the city, feel the emotions, and smell the aroma. What are the different views of the experience? For example, what did Zacchaeus see from the tree? What was the view of the rest of the crowd? What were the emotions expressed? It is important to experience the realities of the story in order to be able to preach and testify from within the experience. In testifying, we reexperience the story as it is being told.[9]

We do not attempt to fake our feelings, but we allow the power of the message to possess us. We allow the power of the message to communicate through our whole being, including our emotions. We are convinced that it is possible to have intellectual integrity and fervor at the same time. Enthusiasm is not the opposite of intelligence. In fact, enthuse is a religious word, *entheos*, that means "full of God." On more than one occasion the critics of Wesley said that he seems to have "good sense, though an enthusiast."

Every public speaker knows the important role the setting plays in the process of communication. Public speaking by its very nature always involves physical realities. These realities provide the matrix for verbalizing the gospel, and they can either enhance or block communication. Sometimes we find ourselves speaking in beautiful buildings that do not enhance communication. We not only find ourselves hidden by large wooden pulpits, but we also find that we are having to speak across a vast space between the pulpit/lectern and the first pew. We have also been in situations where inadequate sound systems and poor acoustics have made communication nearly impossible. The challenges of these situations are magnified when speaking in the open air. Open air witnessing by its very nature confronts the witness with enormous obstacles to communication. Some of these situations can be altered and some cannot, but none of these are as important as how the witness communicates through body language.

Our entire body communicates. Often in our preaching and testifying we are our own worst enemies. As a young boy and his father left church the son said to his father, "Dad, why was the preacher mad?" The father tried to help the young son see that the preacher was simply very intense and felt very strongly about the message. In reality, however, the body language of the speaker communicated anger. Most of us have had the experience of hearing one speak of God's love while clinching the fist and squinting the eyes in anger. The body language contradicts the message of love. Most of us have heard a witness say, "In the name of Jesus, come unto me all you who are tired and weary and I will give you rest," while standing with arms folded. The witness's body language communicates resistance rather than openness or vulnerability.

Often our body language contradicts our words, and if there is a choice, people believe the body! The way the preacher or witness takes the stand will either raise or lower the expectations of the auditors. Dr. Fred Craddock, professor at Candler School of Theology, confirms this key element in effective communication. He writes, "The body is the preacher's instrument for the proclamation of the gospel, not for display but for use."[10] We are not asking a person to fake it, but we are urging that we all allow the gospel to possess us in such a way that the whole body speaks congruently with the words being spoken.

As we get "inside the word and message by seeing and feeling the experience," we are set free by the grace of God to use this marvelous instrument of the human body—

voice, eyes, hands—to communicate the good news of the gospel. Our gestures, emotions, timing, and rhythm will be commensurate with the message as we experience the event and the story anew.

On several occasions we have been asked, "Are effective communicators born or made?" The answer is always the same, yes. For some, this natural use of the body seems to flow easily, but for others it is necessary for them to work at it. How we use this instrument of the body is crucial to the total impact of the message. We have all seen how the message of the witness has been sabotaged by some unconscious action on the part of the speaker. For example, we have all seen speakers who cannot decide if they will keep their glasses on or take them off. We have all watched speakers count money in their pockets or continually button or unbutton their coat. One speaker spent thirty minutes searching for a pocket on his robe! We all may have habits that greatly interfere with the communication of the message.

Hopefully, we have someone who loves us and will tell us what it is we are doing that interferes with the testimony. When a witness takes the stand, leaning back, giving a deep sigh, that witness is communicating a sense of boredom. Soon the hearers will also be in agreement. As Joe Harding reminds us, the very act of the delivery itself is of great importance. More than ninety-three percent of the speaker's communication is at a nonverbal level. These include things such as a tone and inflection of voice, facial expression, physical appearance and energy.[11] We must constantly ask, "What is my body language conveying to the hearer?"

Our Choice of Words

In addition to body language, one's choice of words is of great importance. In the early days of the Methodist movement, John Wesley gave advice to the people who were preaching and testifying. For the most part these were laypersons. Wesley admonished the witnesses to let their language be "plain, proper, and clear."[12] He once wrote to a young lay preacher counseling him to talk in the ordinary language of the people. He advised that as far as possible use one syllable words. Clarity and conciseness were critical principles for Wesley. Particularly, Wesley said he labored to "avoid all words which are not easy to be understood, all which are not used in common life; and in particular, those kinds of technical terms that so frequently occur in Bodies of Divinity."[13]

Cultural Expectations

Another factor in the delivery of the message is the cultural expectation of the hearer. The particular method of delivery must take into consideration the situation of the hearer. Both of us grew up in the Appalachian Mountains where people are known for their folk stories or tales. We grew up among storytellers. From early on, we learned the importance of oral communication. In Appalachia, if the witness believes what he or she is speaking, the witness is able to say it and not read it; if he or she has to read it, the witness does not believe it. Therefore, delivering the message without notes is critical to believability.

There are, however, other situations that demand a written text. Both of us have pastored in communities comprised of people who were primarily government workers, professional people, and university professors. In these situations, if the speaker shows up without a written text, it indicates a serious lack of preparation. The cultural context must be taken seriously by the witness. The manner in which the message is delivered must be appropriate to the occasion, the people, and the gospel itself.

Fred Craddock reminds us that there is a passion that is commensurate to the urgency of the gospel. This passion and sense of urgency is born of a contagion of spirit. We have often asked ourselves, "How did the message of the early church spread so rapidly?" Did it spread by institutions or world systems of propaganda? We have concluded that institutional systems or propaganda had little or nothing to do with the spread of the gospel described in the book of Acts. To the contrary, we believe that the essential dynamic had its birth in the depths of people's souls. This dynamic produced such a contagious spirit that the gospel flew like holy fire from heart to heart. This produced a passion and a sense of urgency that mystified the unbelievers. Therefore, unbelievers were evoked to cry out, "What must I do to be saved?" John Wesley communicated the same contagious spirit, passion and urgency. He was alive in the faith and therefore his message was alive. We would pray to God that the worldwide church could discover this contagion of spirit and passion, which is commensurate to the urgency of the gospel.

When one takes the stand, what could be a greater dynamic for one's witness than this idea proposed by Professor Craddock? There is at least one person present and listening who because of the testimony given may have a "clearer vision, a brighter hope, a deeper faith, a fuller love." That person *is* the witness.[14]

Part Five

Credibility
and Courage of
the Witness

Chapter Twelve

The Word Becomes Flesh

T o this point we have journeyed with the reader along roads that we feel are essential to the theory and practice of Christian preaching and testifying. The journey began with an attempt to establish a firm biblical and theological case for Christian witnessing. Then we made a concerted effort to explain the essentials of the Christian message. Realizing that the Christian gospel does not float somewhere in space, but relates concretely to particular situations, we walked with the reader along the road that leads to a careful consideration of context. This led us to explore a number of practical matters involved in the communication of the gospel. Now we are ready to discuss the important role that credibility and courage play when the redeemed of the Lord witness to their faith.

We preach and testify of the deeds of God in terms of our own autobiography. When we preach and testify, we do so in terms of our own experience. Witnessing is not merely giving a performance, it is giving evidence. One can give a performance as if it were play-acting, but in giving evidence one is willing to stake one's life on the testimony given.

One preaches and testifies about what God has done in terms of one's own story. Thus, one does not speak as if the good news has failed to intersect one's own journey. We dare speak in terms of how the good news has encountered us.

Therefore, our witness is born of personal experience. This is in keeping with what it means to witness. A court of law cannot operate on hearsay. A person who testifies must speak from firsthand experience. According to the law books, a witness presents facts that come within the scope of his or her own knowledge and experience. Each person who is called to the witness stand is called for only one reason, the supposition that some bit of evidence is included in that person's experience. If witnessing is to be meaningful, it must be personal.

To be a Christian witness, one must allow the Word of God to live in one's heart and show forth in one's life. In other words, a person cannot witness to the gospel until God has revealed the Son in him or her. A current bumper sticker has a message that is directly relevant to Christian witnessing. It asks, "If you were arrested for being Christian, would there be enough evidence to convict you?" In this vein, we acknowledge a fundamental weakness of the contemporary church. There are multitudes who are willing to take a balcony seat as mere spectators in the courtroom, but too few are willing to become personally and completely involved by taking the witness stand and giving evidence. The bold act of taking the stand is only for those who are being crucified with Christ, who are experiencing death to their selfish ambitions and strivings and are continually being raised to new life in Christ Jesus.

Testimony, also, involves more than just mountain-top experiences. Some of the most potent testimonies are given from the valley of despair. One day a friend called and shared a situation that was causing great pain in his life. His family had lost a son in a tragic death, a devastating experience for him and his family. During our conversation, he shared that he was being led by God to preach on the scripture, "All things work together for good to those who love God." He said, "I just asked my wife if she believed this word and she responded by saying, 'I want to believe.'"

Often in our testifying we do not always speak as one who is on top of the mountain. We speak as one who goes through the valley of the shadow of death knowing that God is with us. This preacher dared to testify of his faith and his need for faith. We are sure that his congregation will never be quite the same.

The Identity of the Witness

The identity of the one who preaches and testifies is critical. It is no accident that the one who bears testimony is called a witness. In addition, the testimony or body of evidence given is also called witness (e.g., I gave my "witness" at the trial). Also, the act of giving evidence is called witnessing. We hear people say, "He witnessed before the jury." Finally, the word *witness* refers to the act of seeing an event or happening as when one says, "I witnessed the signing of the deed."

Preaching, testifying, or giving evidence have a rich heritage in scripture. We read, "When the Holy Spirit has come upon you . . . you will be my witnesses" (Acts 1:8). Paul declares to the early church: "I do not account my life of any value to myself, if only I may finish my course and the ministry I received from the Lord Jesus, to testify to the good news of God's grace" (Acts 20:24).

The identity of the witness (the one who testifies) can be seen by utilizing the imagery of the law court. By way of that imagery we perceive who the witness is. First, we see that the witness is not the judge. This is a word of warning to those preachers and lay witnesses who tend to get confused in their roles. Jesus is quite clear in his admonition: "Do not judge so that you may not be judged" (Matt. 7:1). We have the uncanny tendency to usurp God's role in judgment. We want to separate the wheat from the tares and the sheep from the goats. Every preacher and lay witness need to hear the words, "Who made you a judge?"

Second, the witness is not the prosecuting attorney. This represents those persons who are bent on seeing to it that people get exactly what they deserve. When the witness is tempted in this direction, he or she must ask the question, "What if I should receive from the hand of God exactly what I deserve at this moment in time? Would I be content?"

Third, the witness is not the defending attorney. This may sound contradictory; after all, haven't we said that it is necessary for the church to make a case for the gospel in this skeptical world? We hope that we are not splitting hairs at this point, but it seems to us that there is a fundamental difference between advancing the gospel of the kingdom through preaching and testifying—through persuasion and demonstration—or by going on the defensive. Defensiveness is usually born of a posture of insecurity, fear, and threat. Where there is faith, hope, love, and a willingness to risk the church goes on the offensive. Therefore, the posture of the witness is quite different from a siege mentality that makes the church defensive. There are so many threats to the church's life both in the world and from within the congregation that we are tempted to take a defensive posture and become negative defenders of the faith, rather than positive witnesses of an event that was nothing less than God breaking into the world, transforming human life and all creation. We have seen who the witness *is not*. It is now necessary to state who the witness *is*.

In a court trial the aim is to discover truth. A witness is asked to take the stand and testify in order to get at the truth. Thomas Long, Professor of Preaching at Princeton, insists that the forensic metaphor used to define a witness gives it great power:

The witness is in every way one of the people but he or she is placed on the witness stand because of two credentials: The witness has seen something and the witness is willing to tell the truth about it—the whole truth and nothing but the truth.[1]

In discovering truth and justice, the witness is a means toward that end. As such, the personal attributes of the witness may seem rather unimportant. In reality, the identity and character of the witness is of critical significance. Long writes, "If the witness lies—bears false witness—the ability of the people to discover the truth suffers a grievous blow."[2]

The Ten Commandments forbid the bearing of false witness (Exod. 20:16). The giving of false testimony is fatal in the exercise of freedom and justice. Perjury or lying is not tolerated in the halls of justice. Moreover, the very life of the witness is bound with the credibility of the testimony given. Long points out that when the truth given by the witness is despised by the people, the witness may be hurt or even killed. "It is no coincidence that the New Testament word for witness is *martyr*."[3]

There are several important observations involved in understanding the identity of the witness.[4] First, the one who preaches and testifies has authority not because of office or rank, but because of what that person has seen and heard. The Christian testifies to the God revealed in scripture and to the God who is alive and at work in the world. Second, the witness testifies regarding his or her own personal encounter with God. Third, the witness tells his or her own story and how that story corresponds with the events of God's revelation. Therefore, the witness is not a neutral observer. The witness has experienced the event itself and is intimately involved in the message. Our lives do matter. For a public witness, morality is never private. Our lifestyles are not only relevant to our message, they confirm and illumine the message.

The importance of the character of the speaker is not a new idea. Aristotle taught that the *ethos* of the speaker was a vital element in the power of persuasion.[5] For him *ethos* consisted of good sense, good character, and good will toward the audience itself. According to Aristotle, a powerful witness is characterized by these elements: competency, character, and compassion. In preaching and testifying, the message and the one who witnesses are inextricably bound together. We cannot act as if the story of God has never intersected our story. In preaching and testifying the Word becomes flesh.

One of our very special friends, the Reverend Olav Parnamets, is superintendent of The Methodist Church in Estonia, a Soviet occupied Baltic nation. The church in Estonia is a great witness to the power of the gospel. During the last fifty years the people have lived faithfully at great risk. The former superintendent of The Methodist Church in the 1940's was taken to Siberia and executed. A successor superintendent was later sentenced to hard labor in Siberia and served there more than five years. Laity and clergy in the Soviet Union have known the meaning of costly discipleship over the last half-century. They were not allowed to have Christian education, but they were allowed to have choirs because the choirs were considered cultural (the leaders said they had many choirs). Since they were not allowed to have house-church meetings, they would gather in homes in order to celebrate a member's birthday. As Olav Parnamets has often said, "When you are living in a lion's den, you learn to do so without stepping on the lion's tail."

For several years in the late 1970s we longed to have Olav come to visit us. Numerous invitations were issued on behalf of church agencies. His government always refused to grant permission. Finally, in desperation we were advised to try the "kitchen door technique," that is, invite him personally and not officially. We remember writing on plain white paper, not official stationery, and inviting Olav to come to the United States and visit us. We wrote, "We would love to have you visit us. Now come and see us, you hear." That is about as unofficial as you get! Olav took our invitation to the officials and they said, "Go." He could not believe it and neither could we. We asked him to call when he arrived in New York. On the day of his arrival, there was no call. However, we went to the airport to meet Olav, not knowing whether or not he would be on the plane. We wondered if he had been detained at the last moment. After all, he had been denied permission many times.

As the plane taxied to the gate, we prayed that Olav would be on it. People came streaming off the plane, but there was no sign of Olav. Our hearts sank. We were sure Olav had not come, but just at that moment a very powerful looking man wearing a fur hat was standing in the doorway of the plane. There was no question, it had to be Olav. As he came down the stairway I called, "Olav."

"Ed-die!"

We met and Olav exclaimed, "It is a miracle." We all hugged one another. It is not often that speech eludes me, but at that moment I could only say, "It is indeed a miracle."

During the week we learned of the many challenges that Olav and his people constantly face in their witness to the gospel. Olav was one of a number of New World Missioners from around the globe whom we had invited to the United States of America to preach the gospel in churches across our country. At the end of our week together, we always end with a service of worship. In that service we pray for one another and receive Holy Communion. The New World Missioners select one of their members to speak on their behalf and, of course, they selected Olav. He was very nervous. He had never spoken in English in a public meeting. As he walked to the front, there was a long awkward moment while he searched for a particular verse of scripture in the English version of the Bible. Finally, he found what he was looking for in the Bible, and he began reading: "Thus says the Lord to his anointed, to Cyrus . . . I will go before you and level the mountains, I will break in pieces the doors of bronze and cut through the bars of iron" (Isa. 45:1, 2). There was a long pause and afterward Olav looked up and said, "Sometimes those iron bars are called the 'Iron Curtain.' "

It was an electrifying moment! People experienced the active presence of the living God. A passage of scripture came alive! Why? The Word became flesh. Olav dared to speak as one who experienced the living God who leads him and his people. Now that we have witnessed the crumbling of the Iron Curtain, we remember Olav's announcement of One who cuts through iron bars. It is an echo of Psalm 107. The Psalmist invites us to sing the doxology in gratitude for the steadfast love of the Lord whose wonderful works to humankind are made manifest. In verse 16 we read, "For he shatters the doors of bronze, and cuts in two the bars of iron." What greater call to witness could there be than: "Let the redeemed of the Lord say so, those he redeemed from trouble" (Ps. 107:2).

Chapter Thirteen

The Courage to Keep On

Once the Spirit nudges us into this adventure of preaching and testifying, what is it that keeps us going?

one of the favorite places to visit in the United States is the Smithsonian Institution in Washington, D.C. One could spend days there and still not see all there is to see. A very special part of the Institution is the Air and Space Museum.

At the museum one is surrounded with the vehicles of space—the Glenn capsule, *Gemini*, and the space lab. Near the front entrance is the original airplane invented by the Wright Brothers. Overhead is the very famous little plane, *The Spirit of St. Louis*, and one marvels at the journey of Lindbergh. Just behind Lindbergh's plane is the exhibit that many people wish to see, the *Voyager*.

The story behind the *Voyager* is incredible. It looks like a flying petrol tank. It has drooping wings on either side of a tiny cockpit. This clumsy-looking craft and its two pilots recorded a remarkable aviation achievement. Two days before Christmas, 1986, after completing the first non-stop global atmospheric flight without refueling, pilots Dick Rutan and Jeana Yeager landed this plane in the Mojave Desert in California. We recall their journey and how each day their location was given by the media. All persons in the aviation

field acknowledged these pilots, and their plane, for they
recorded an amazing accomplishment.

As always, there was a press conference and interviews.
Someone asked if their journey was ever in jeopardy. Did
they ever consider landing short of their destination? How
were they able to endure the cramped quarters of the tiny
cockpit? Did they think at anytime they might have to quit
and give up their dream and goal? One of them answered, "At
times we almost gave up. But we kept going because of the
people who had helped us and the unconquerable faith that
we could complete the journey."

The questions posed by the press are old questions, and yet
they are new questions. How do people keep going when the
going is tough? That is a question in the Old Testament, and
that is a question in the New Testament.

In the Old Testament there is the story of Nehemiah. His
homeland is conquered and he is carted away as a hostage in a
foreign land. He is homesick. One day a benevolent king
releases him from exile and immediately he sets out for his
hometown. Upon arrival in Jerusalem, he discovers that his
city is in shambles. Even the wall around the city,the very
symbol of its existence, is in ruins. It is hard to imagine what
the prophet was feeling. It would be easy for him to join the
community of despair and acquiesce to the situation.
Instead, he sets out to rebuild the wall of the city of
Jerusalem. He reaches for a stone and puts it in place. Then
he places another and another until he is on the wall. People
pass by and taunt him. "What are you doing, man?" "You
will never live to see it finished. You might as well give it up,
come on down." Notice the answer of the prophet to those
who are taunting him and challenging him: "I cannot come
down. I am doing a great work and I cannot come down"
(Neh. 6:3).

What is it that keeps people from giving up their work and
coming down from the wall? Hardly anyone who has been

involved with the ministry of preaching and testifying for any length of time has not been tempted to come down from the wall. When the witness looks at the enormity of the challenge and the taunting of those who dish out discouragement, the temptation to leave the wall is real and persistent. What gives witnesses the courage to keep on going?

Believing in One's Task

The answer can be found in listening to the pilots, the prophets, and the apostles. The pilots said, "We remembered what we were doing and we believed we could finish the journey." The prophet thundered, "I am doing a great thing and I will not come down."

When we begin losing the conviction that preaching and testifying make a difference, we grow weary and are tempted to quit. It is the conviction that witnessing is of ultimate significance that keeps us going. Let any preacher or lay witness begin to think that preaching and witnessing do not make a difference and they will not.

Earlier we noted the importance of confidence in the transforming power of the gospel. Any loss of that confidence is enough to cause persons to surrender the task. In writing to the Corinthian church, Paul speaks of a great boldness and confidence that is born of steadfast hope. He knows the gospel he preaches has the power to transform people, "from one degree of glory to another" (2 Cor. 3:18).

The gospel is the power that transforms human lives and society. It is important to hold this confidence and to have it consistently and constantly reinforced in our experience. Recently we were attending a World Methodist Evangelism Institute at the Juan Wesley Seminario in Monterey, Mexico. Since we were having lectures in both Spanish and English, the Institute had employed a professional translator to interpret the lectures simultaneously over electronic head-sets. In a lecture in which we were illustrating how to tell a story, we were using the legendary story "Tie a Yellow Ribbon 'Round the Old Oak Tree":

> A young son leaves home and lives a life that results in his being imprisoned. As the time comes for him to be released, he writes his father and mother a letter in which he tells them that he knows that he has brought shame to them and the family. He states that he would understand if they did not want him to come back home. The letter then tells them that on a particular day he is planning to be on the train back to their hometown. Because the train goes by the family home, the boy writes his mother and father, "If you want me to come home, tie a yellow ribbon 'round the old oak tree behind the house."
>
> The day arrives and the boy's heart is pounding. Finally, he relates his story to the man sitting next to him on the train. He points out that they are almost there and that he is unable to look for himself. He requests that the stranger look for him. As the train rounds the bend, the man lifts the boy's face and declares, "Look, boy, look! There's a yellow ribbon on every limb!"[6]

Until this moment we could hear the translator's voice through the headsets, but suddenly the headsets went silent. Thinking he did not understand, the last statement was repeated more loudly, "Look, boy, look! There's a yellow ribbon on every limb." Still there was no sound. Again, the final line was repeated only to notice the interpreter had removed his headset, and he was weeping. He had heard a new word about the God who forgives and reconciles, and he was moved deeply in his soul. The setting was a lecture hall, but in a moment the Spirit had led a person to encounter the reality of God.

When we experience the power of the gospel to transform and change people again and again, we are renewed by the Spirit and encouraged to continue preaching and testifying. We find ourselves exclaiming, "I am doing a great work. I cannot come down from the wall. I will not come down."

Others Believe in Us

Another dynamic that enabled the pilots, the prophets, and the apostles to keep going was the fact that they remembered those who had confidence in them. Nehemiah remembered those who were counting on him to build the wall, and he could not quit. The pilots remembered those who had helped put them into orbit, and they refused to land short of their goal. Paul remembered those who were counting on him to bring the gospel message to Corinth and he refused to lose heart.

We discovered very early in our ministry that if we could find persons who believed in us and were willing to stand with us, we could do it. What we could not endure was to be alone. There is tremendous power unleashed when people believe in you and are willing to stand with you.

In 1924 an Olympic champion was traveling around the United States speaking to elementary and high school students. In Cleveland, Ohio, a young skinny kid asked the champion, "Do you think I could be an Olympic champion?" The champion replied, "Yes I do, and if you and God decide it, you can be." Twelve years later that same scrawny little kid named Jesse Owens won the 1936 Olympics in Berlin, in front of and in spite of, a man named Hitler. He was inspired to accomplish the impossible because there was someone who knew him and believed in him.

In the film titled "Productivity: Self-Fulfilling Prophecy," produced by McGraw-Hill, a very interesting story is related. A professor of education named Rosenthal decided to conduct an experiment with teachers. He indicated that a certain group of students in the teacher's class had been selected because they had tested high and were expected to excel as students. The truth was that all the young children were selected at random. The only difference was in the mind of the teacher. At the end of the experiment the children whom the teacher expected to excel did excel. One or two of the children who were not in the selected group excelled nonetheless. However, the teacher seemed unhappy with them. Rosenthal concluded that people tend to live up to expectations held by key persons who surround them.

We have a way of making people become what we believe them to be. One of the authors remembers two of his high school teachers very well. One teacher was neurotic. He would give an examination and proceed to prowl up and down the aisles in his attempt to catch cheaters. He would move behind you, grab your hand, and push up your coat sleeve to see if you had anything written on your shirt cuffs. He would even examine the white rubber soles on your tennis shoes. There were students in that class who would cheat just in order to see if they could outdo this neurotic teacher.

The other teacher was an elderly woman named Docia Vandevanter whom the students loved. She was weak and frail, but she continued to teach because of her commitment to the students. She always wrote her exams on the board, and she would say, "Now students, I had a difficult night last night and I am so tired. While you write your exams, I will go next door and drink a cup of hot tea. I know that you would not do anything to disappoint my expectations of you. You know how I love you." She would leave the room. There were students who would fail their exam rather than borrow someone else's answers. And do you know why George Morris knows that? *Love ennobles the ignoble by believing the best.*

It matters if someone believes in you. When one of the authors, Eddie Fox, was elected as Director of World Evangelism, he received many letters from around the world. The work and ministry of World Evangelism was held in great regard by church leaders and others because of their respect for the World Methodist Council and the Reverend Dr. Sir Alan Walker of Australia, predecessor in this office. All of these letters of encouragement were treasured, including a very meaningful letter from Dr. Billy Graham.

One letter however was very special. It came from Aunt Mary. She grew up and lived all of her life in a small mountain home nestled in the hollow of the beautiful Appalachian Mountains. She ate, talked, and thought as an Appalachian dweller. She had no idea about the bureaucracy of The United Methodist Church and knew next to nothing about the World Methodist Council. Upon learning of the new appointment Aunt Mary wrote saying, "Dear Son, I hear you have changed jobs. Son, I know that many will come to know Jesus because of what you do." Recalling her letter helps this author to continue preaching and testifying.

Hopefully, all of us are fortunate in having our "Aunt Marys" and "Mrs. Vandevanters." They believe in us, expect the best of us, and stand beside us. It is this ministry of encouragement that sustains us and keeps us from losing heart. We need the support and encouragement of those in the community of faith. When we remember those who believe in us, we exclaim, "We cannot come down from the wall. We will not come down!"

God Believes in Us

Paul makes clear the basis of our primary encouragement: "Since it is by God's mercy that we are engaged in this ministry, we do not lose heart" (2 Cor. 4:1). God believes in us and has given us the power to do this ministry. The Bible makes it clear that God believes in us and holds high expectations of us. One powerful New Testament passage reads:

> But you are a chosen race
> a royal priesthood, a holy nation
> God's own people,
> In order that you may proclaim

the mighty acts of him who called
you out of darkness into his marvelous light.
Once you were not a people
but now you are God's people;
once you had not received mercy
but now you have received mercy.

(1 Pet. 2:9-10)

Because of God's grace, we are no longer nobodies, we are somebodies! We are not orphaned in an impersonal universe. We are now constituted as God's own people to do God's own will in God's own way. We are living in a time of tremendous challenge. Never has the need for preaching and testifying been greater. Recently an article in the *Wall Street Journal* (February 15, 1989) reported that a special shoe was developed for the thousands of people who walk in indoor malls for exercise. According to the article, the shoe is "designed to give extra traction for smoother, slicker mall floors." The shoe is designed so as to "propel the body's momentum forward." These are the kinds of shoes needed by those of us called to testify and preach.

When we look at this world and the people who are hurting, lonely, and enslaved, it is no time for us to lean back. It is time for us to be propelled forward. Paul, writing to the people of Macedonia, sets the spiritual pace for our advance. He says, "Forgetting what lies behind and straining forward to what lies ahead, I press on toward the goal for the prize of the heavenly call of God in Christ Jesus" (Phil. 3:13*b*-14). When we remember who we are and whose we are and those who believe in us, we take courage and are motivated to share the good news of Christ. We cannot come down from the wall. The eternal gospel lures us forward with an everlasting hope, and the Holy Spirit empowers us to be witnesses "in Jerusalem, in all Judea and Samaria, and to the ends of the earth" (Acts 1:8).

The tiny kingdom of Tonga in the South Pacific is one of
the happiest and most wholesome countries in the world.
With a population of 100,000 people living in thirty small
island communities, it is only a dot in the vast Pacific Ocean.
Located just west of the International Date Line, day begins
in Tonga. The country has a very small police and military
force as there is little crime. Tonga is ruled by a king who is a
committed Christian and a lay preacher in the Free
Wesleyan (Methodist) Church. Tonga is known throughout
the world as the friendly islands. To visit there is to
experience a hospitality that is equalled scarcely anywhere
else in the world. Tongans are a strong gentle people who
value family life, and who are bound together in responsible
community structures. Beyond any doubt, at the very heart
of life in the kingdom of Tonga is the Christian church. To
visit   to find oneself asking "How on earth did such a
pla   ?" This question cannot be answered without
r   n infinitesimally small village called 'Utui.

          ;e of approximately three hundred persons, is
          iles from Neiafu, the capital of the northern
      nds called Vava'u in the kingdom of Tonga. On
    , a miracle happened in 'Utui which was to have
    n the entire South Pacific. A group of faithful
    Christians gathered in a field near the village to
    ay. During this prayer meeting, the people
    a Pentecostal visitation. The Holy Spirit came
    ople with such power that the entire community
    rmed. People were set afire in this "Tongan
    to spread the gospel throughout the entire
    Tonga. The church grew with amazing rapidity.
    gations were established throughout the king-

    'ongans climbed into their sea-going canoes, and
    ;tal power pushed them 500 miles to the west to
    ;pel with their Fijian neighbors. A year later they

journeyed by sea 300 miles north to Samoa to witness the gospel to their former bitter enemies. This is one of the most remarkable stories in the history of missionary activity.

Today if you travel to 'Utui, you will find one of the most unusual historical markers in the world. As far as we know, it is the only monument erected to commemorate the visitation of the Holy Spirit! During the writing of this book, the two of us traveled together to 'Utui.

We wanted to kneel on this holy ground in order to pray for a fresh outpouring of the Holy Spirit and a World Pentecost. Our study of church history has taught us that there was a Jerusalem Pentecost, a Wesleyan Pentecost, and a Tongan Pentecost. We believe the time is ripe for a World Pentecost.

One of the most moving moments of our lives came at a great open-air service on January 20, 1991, at 'Utui. After a sermon on the need for the baptism of the Holy Spirit, the two of us knelt before the marker commemorating the Tongan Pentecost and asked leaders of The Methodist Church of Tonga to lay hands on us and pray that God would empower us to fulfill the ministry to which God has called us. While the leaders were praying, spontaneously, women and men of 'Utui came forward and fell prostrate on the ground. They began to pray fervently for us and a World Pentecost. After a long season of prayer, people from 'Utui and the region came forward and asked us to lay hands on them for the receiving of the Holy Spirit. Miraculously, the spirit of revival began anew at 'Utui. In subsequent days, we experienced the same outpouring of the Holy Spirit at Neiafu, Ha'apai, and 'Eua. People responded by the hundreds and came forward to receive the Holy Spirit and commit themselves to witnessing to their faith.

This experience has confirmed for us the conviction that we are in the dawning stages of a new World Pentecost that is producing a new world missionary movement. All over the world the Spirit is moving, giving people the courage and the power to preach and testify. More and more people are obeying the Spirit, and like the psalmist are declaring, *Let the Redeemed of the Lord Say So!* It is our prayer that the reader will become a part of this new missionary movement.

Notes

Introduction

1. Emilio Castro, *International Bulletin of Missionary Research*, Volume XIV, No. 4, October 1990, p. 146.

Part One: A Case for Preaching and Testifying

1. Gallup Report, *The Unchurched American Ten Years Later*, The Princeton Religion Research Center, 1988, pp. 3-4.
2. William Barclay, *Turning to God* (Grand Rapids: Baker Book House), 1964, p. 31.
3. Michael Green, *Evangelism in the Early Church* (Grand Rapids: Eerdmans, 1970), p. 173.
4. Howard A. Snyder, *Liberating the Church* (Downers Grove: InterVarsity Press, 1975), p. 116.
5. C. H. Dodd, *Apostolic Preaching and Its Development* (New York: Harper and Row, 1936).
6. Robert C. Worley, *Preaching and Teaching in the Earliest Church* (Philadelphia: Westminster, 1967), pp. 35-36.
7. Allison A. Trites, *The New Testament Concept of Witness*, pp. 15, 16, 223-227.
8. Pope Paul IV, No. 24, *Evangelii Nuntiandi*.
9. Thomas G. Long, *The Witness of Preaching* (Louisville: Westminster, 1989), p. 78.
10. William E. Sangster, *Power in Preaching*, (Nashville: Abingdon, 1958), p. 21.
11. *The Works of John Wesley*, Vol. 1 (Grand Rapids: Baker House), p. 185.
12. Ibid., p. 18.
13. David Martin, *The Breaking of the Image* (New York: St. Martin's Press, 1979), p. 81.
14. *The Works of John Wesley*, Vol. 1, p. 186.
15. Ibid. Vol. XIII, p. 258.
16. John R. W. Scott, *Christian Mission* (Downers Grove: InterVarsity Press, 1975), pp. 59, 60.
17. Leander E. Keck, *The Bible in the Pulpit* (Nashville: Abingdon, 1978), pp. 38, ff.
18. David H. C. Read, *Sent From God* (Nashville: Abingdon, 1974), p. 12.
19. David Martin, *The Breaking of the Image* (New York: St. Martin's Press, 1979), pp. 103-118.
20. Alvin Toffler, *Future Shock* (New York: Random House, 1970).
21. *The Atlanta Journal and Constitution*, 29 April 1990, Sun.

182   Let the Redeemed of the Lord Say So!

22. Paul Scherer, *For We Have This Treasure* (Grand Rapids: Baker, 1976), p. 28.
23. Ibid.
24. Fred Craddock, *Overhearing the Gospel* (Nashville: Abingdon, 1978), p. 14.
25. Karl Barth, *Church Dogmatics*, Vol. 4, #3, (Edinburgh: T. and T. Clark, 1962), pp. 561-614.
26. Orlando Costas, *Christ Outside the Gate* (Maryknoll: Orbis Books, 1982), p. 80.
27. Leander Keck, *The Bible in the Pulpit* (Nashville: Abingdon, 1978), p. 11.

Part Two: Content of Preaching and Testifying

1. Emilio Castro, *International Bulletin of Missionary Research*, Volume XIV, No. 4, October 1990, p. 146.
2. Norman Perrin, *Jesus and the Language of the Kingdom: Symbol and Metaphor in New Testament Interpretation* (Philadelphia: Fortress Press, 1976), pp. 29-32. or
   Mortimer Arias, *Announcing the Reign of God: Evangelization and the Subversive Memory of Jesus*, (Philadelphia: Fortress Press, 1984).
3. David Martin, *The Breaking of the Image* (New York: St. Martin's Press, 1979), p. 76.
4. John H. Sammis, "Trust and Obey," *The United Methodist Hymnal*, (Nashville: The United Methodist Publishing House), p. 467.
5. Norman Perrin, *The Kingdom of God in the Teaching of Jesus* (London: SCM Press, 1963), p. 162.
6. D. T. Niles, *Preaching the Gospel of the Resurrection* (Philadelphia: Westminster, 1954), p. 28.
7. Michael Green, *Evangelism in the Early Church* (Grand Rapids: Eerdmans, 1970), pp. 150-151.
8. Aflred C. Krass, *Evangelizing Neopagan North America* (Scottsdale: The Herald Press, 1982), pp. 28-29.
9. Gerhard Kittel, ed., *Theological Dictionary of the New Testament*, Vol. 1 (Grand Rapids: Eerdmans Publishing Company, 1976), p. 583.
10. John Wesley did not completely affirm the contribution that Constantine's conversion brought to Christianity. See Theodore W. Jennings, Jr., *Good News to the Poor* (Nashville: Abingdon, 1990), pp. 38-43.
11. Albert Outler, *The Works of John Wesley*, Vol. V, No. 1 (Nashville: Abingdon, 1984), p. 98.
12. Albert Outler, *Sermons On the Way to the Kingdom*, Vol. V., No. 1, p. 232.
13. Ibid., p. 224.
14. Ibid., p. 17.
15. Ibid., p. 98.
16. H. Eddie Fox, George E. Morris, *Faith Sharing* (Nashville: Discipleship Resources, 1986), pp. 105-111.
17. W. L. Doughty, *John Wesley, Preacher* (London: Epworth Press, 1955), p. 209.
18. Paul Waitman Hoon, *The Integrity of Worship* (Nashville: Abingdon, 1971), p. 75.
19. Michael Green, *Evangelism in the Early Church*, p. 151.
20. William D. Maxwell, *An Outline of Christian Worship* (London: Oxford University Press, 1936), p. 12.
21. Paul Scherer, *The Word God Sent* (New York: Harper and Row, 1965), pp. 24-25.

22. Jurgen Moltmann, *The Church in the Power of the Spirit* (New York: Harper & Row, 1977), p. 77.
23. P. T. Forsyth, *Positive Preaching and the Modern Mind* (London: Independent Press, 1949), pp. 6, 22.
24. John R. Claypool, *The Preaching Event* (San Francisco: Harper and Row, 1989), p. 29.
25. Ibid., p. 31.
26. Dietrich Bonhoeffer, *The Cost of Discipleship* (New York: Macmillan, 1949), p. 225.
27. Emil Brunner, *Truth As Encounter* (Philadelphia: Westminster Press, 1964), p. 49.
28. Ibid., p. 114.
29. George Morris, *The Mystery and Meaning of Christian Conversion* (Nashville: Discipleship Resources), pp. 59-60.
30. David H. C. Read, *Sent From God* (Nashville: Abingdon, 1974), p. 80.

Part Three: Context for Preaching and Testifying

1. George Morris, *Mystery and Meaning of Christian Conversion* (Nashville: Discipleship Resources), pp. 11-12.

Part Four: Communicating the Gospel

1. H. Eddie Fox and George E. Morris, *Faith-Sharing* (Nashville: Discipleship Resources, 1986), pp. 233-36.
2. Leighton Ford, "How to Give an Honest Invitation," *Leadership*, Vol. V, No. 2, Spring 1984, p. 105.
3. Raymond H. Bailey, "Ethics in Preaching," *Review and Expositor*, 86, 1989, pp. 541, 543.
4. Maxie D. Dunnam, *The Communicators Commentary*, Vol. 8 (Waco, Texas: Word Books, 1982), p. 122.
5. O. Dean Martin, *Invite: Preaching for Response* (Nashville: Discipleship Resources), p. 65.
6. Alan Walker, *Stand Up to Preach* (Nashville: Discipleship Resources), p. 66.
7. Ibid., p. 64.
8. O. Dean Martin, *Invite: Preaching for Response* (Nashville: Discipleship Resources), p. 66.
9. Joe Harding, *Have I Told You Lately?* (Pasadena: Church Growth Press, 1962), p. 31.
10. Fred Craddock, *Preaching* (Nashville: Abingdon, 1985), p. 214.
11. Ibid., p. 34.
12. W. C. Doughty, *John Wesley Preacher* (London: The Epworth Press, 1955), p. 141.
13. Ibid., p. 143.
14. Fred Craddock, *Preaching* (Nashville: Abingdon, 1985), p. 222.

Part Five: Credibility and Courage of the Witness

1. Thomas Long, *The Witness of Preaching* (Louisville: Westminster Press, 1989), p. 43.
2. Ibid.

3. Ibid., p. 44.
4. Ibid., pp. 44-47.
5. Wayne Thompson, *The Process of Persuasion* (New York: Harper and Row, 1975), pp. 59-62.
6. H. Eddie Fox, *Grace-Esteem* (Nashville: Discipleship Resources 1988), pp. 8-9.

Suggested Reading

Abraham, William J. *The Logic of Evangelism: The Creed, Spiritual Gifts, and Disciplines*. Grand Rapids: W. B. Eerdmans, 1989.

Arias, Mortimer. *Announcing the Reign of God: Evangelization and the Subversive Memory of Jesus*. Philadelphia: Fortress Press, 1984.

Armstrong, Richard Stoll. *The Pastor As Evangelist*. Philadelphia: Westminster Press, 1984.

Barclay, William. *Turning to God*. Grand Rapids: Baker Book House, 1964.

Barth, Karl. *Church Dogmatics*. Edinburgh: T. and T. Clark, 1962, Vol. 4. #3.

Bonhoeffer, Dietrich. *The Cost of Discipleship*. New York: Macmillan, 1949.

Bosch, David J. *Witness to the World*. Atlanta: John Knox Press, 1980.

Brewer, Earl D. C., and Scott L. Thumma. *World Methodism and World Issues*. Atlanta: The Center for Religious Research, 1990.

Brunner, Emil. *Truth as Encounter*. Philadelphia: Westminster Press, 1964.

Castro, Emilio. *Sent Free: Mission and Unity in the Perspective of the Kingdom*. Grand Rapids: Eerdmans, 1985.

Childress, James F., and David B. Harned. *Secularization and the Protestant Prospect*. Philadelphia: Westminster Press, 1970.

Claypool, John R. *The Preaching Event*. San Francisco: Harper and Row, 1989.

Costas, Orlando E. *Christ Outside the Gates*. New York: Orbis Books, 1982.

————. *Liberating News: A Theology of Contextual Evangelization*. Grand Rapids: W. B. Eerdmans, 1989.

Cowell, James W. *Extending Your Congregation's Welcome*. Nashville: Discipleship Resources, 1989.

Craddock, Fred. *Overhearing the Gospel*. Nashville: Abingdon Press, 1978.

————. *Preaching*. Nashville: Abingdon Press, 1985.

Dodd, C. H. *Apostolic Preaching and Its Development*. New York: Harper and Row, 1936.

Donovan, Vincent J. *Christianity Rediscovered*. Maryknoll, New York: Orbis Books, 1978.

Dorr, Luther M. *The Bivocational Pastor*. Nashville: Broadman Press, 1988.

Doughty, W. L. *John Wesley, Preacher*. London: Epworth Press, 1955.

Dunnam, Maxie. *The Communicators Commentary*. Waco, Texas: Word Books, 1982, Vol. 8.

English, Donald. *Why Believe in Jesus?* London: Epworth Press, 1986.

_____. *God In the Gallery*. London: Epworth Press, 1975.

Forsyth, P. T. *Positive Preaching and the Modern Mind*. London: Independent Press, 1949.

Fox, H. Eddie. *Grace-Esteem*. Nashville: Discipleship Resources, 1988.

Fox, H. Eddie, and George E. Morris. *Faith-Sharing*. Nashville: Discipleship Resources, 1986.

Gallup, George, Jr. *The Unchurched American Ten Years Later*. Princeton, N.J.: The Princeton Religion Research Center, 1988.

Greeley, Andrew M. *Unsecular Man*. New York: Dell Publishing, 1974.

Green, Michael. *Evangelism in the Early Church*. Grand Rapids: W. B. Eerdmans, 1970.

Haines, J. Harry. *Committed Locally—Living Globally*. Nashville: Abingdon Press, 1982.

Hale, Joe. *Design for Evangelism*. Nashville: Tidings, 1969.

Harding, Joe. *Have I Told You Lately?* Pasadena: Church Growth Press, 1982.

Hauerwas, Stanley, and William H. Willimon. *Resident Aliens*. Nashville: Abingdon Press, 1989.

Henderson, Robert T. *Joy to the World*. Atlanta: John Knox Press, 1980.

Hinson, William H. *A Place to Dig In: Doing Evangelism in the Local Church*. Nashville: Abingdon Press, 1987.

Holsinger, James W., Jr., and Evelyn Laycock. *Awakening the Giant*. Nashville: Abingdon Press, 1989.

Hunter, George G., III. *To Spread the Power: Church Growth in the Wesleyan Spirit*. Nashville: Abingdon Press, 1987.

Jennings, Theodore W., Jr., *Good News to the Poor*. Nashville: Abingdon Press, 1990.

Keck, Leander E. *The Bible in the Pulpit*. Nashville: Abingdon Press, 1978.

Kittel, Gerhard, ed. *Theological Dictionary of the New Testament*. Grand Rapids: W. B. Eerdmans, 1976.

Kraft, Charles H. *Communication Theory for Christian Witness*. Nashville: Abingdon Press, 1983.

Krass, Alfred C. *Evangelizing Neopagan North America*. Scottsdale, Pennsylvania: the Herald Press, 1982.

Long, Thomas. *The Witness of Preaching.* Louisville, KY: Westminister Press, 1989.

Martin, David. *The Breaking of the Image.* New York: St. Martin's Press, 1979.

Martin, O. Dean. *Invite: Preaching for Response.* Nashville: Discipleship Resources, 1987.

Maxwell, William D. *An Outlining of Christian Worship.* London: Oxford University Press, 1936.

Messer, Donald E. *Images of Christian Ministry.* Nashville: Abingdon Press, 1989.

Miles, Delos. *Overcoming Barriers to Witnessing.* Nashville: Broadman Press, 1984.

Moltmann, Jurgen. *The Church in the Power of the Spirit.* New York: Harper and Row, 1977.

Morris, George E. *The Mystery and Meaning of Christian Conversion.* Nashville: Discipleship Resources, 1981.

New Life Mission Handbook. Nashville: Discipleship Resources.

Newbigin, Lesslie. *Foolishness to the Greeks,* Grand Rapids: Eerdmans, 1986.

Niles, David Thambyrajah. *Preaching the Gospel of the Resurrection.* Philadelphia: Westminster Press, 1954.

Oden, Thomas C. *After Modernity . . . What?* Grand Rapids: Zondervan, 1990.

Outler, Albert C. (ed) *The Works of John Wesley—Vols. I-IV.* Nashville: Abingdon Press, 1984–87.

Padilla, René C. *Mission Between the Times: Essays on the Kingdom.* Grand Rapids: W. B. Eerdmans, 1985.

Perrin, Norman. *Jesus and the Language of the Kingdom: Symbol and Metaphor in New Testament Interpretation.* Philadelphia: Fortress Press, 1976.

————. *The Kingdom of God in the Teaching of Jesus.* London: SCM Press, 1963.

Pixley, George. *God's Kingdom: A Guide for Biblical Study:* Maryknoll, New York: translated by Donald Walsh, Orbis Books, 1981.

Read, David H. C. *Sent from God.* Nashville: Abingdon Press, 1974.

————. *Preaching About the Needs of Real People.* Philadelphia: Westminster Press, 1988.

Sangster, William E. *Power in Preaching.* Nashville: Abingdon Press, 1958.

Scherer, Paul. *For We Have This Treasure.* Grand Rapids: Baker Book House, 1976.

————. *The Word God Sent.* New York: Harper and Row, 1965.

Schrieter, Robert J. *Constructing Local Theologies.* Maryknoll, New York: Oribs Books, 1985.

Snyder, Howard A. *Liberating the Church*. Downers Grove, Ill.: InterVarsity Press, 1983.

————. *Signs of the Spirit*. Grand Rapids: Zondervan, 1989.

Stott, John R. W. *Christian Mission in the Modern World*. Downer Grove, Ill.: InterVarsity Press, 1975.

Stott, John R. W., and Robert Coote. *Down to Earth: Studies in Christianity and Culture*. Grand Rapids: W. B. Eerdmans, 1980.

Toffler, Alvin. *Future Shock*. New York: Bantam Books, 1970.

Trites, Allison A. *The New Testament Concept of Witness*. Cambridge, England: Cambridge University Press, 1977.

Von Rad, Gerhard. *Biblical Interpretations in Preaching*. Nashville: Abingdon Press, 1977.

Waitman Hoon, Paul. *The Integrity of Worship*. Nashville: Abingdon Press, 1971.

Walker, Alan. *Standing Up to Preach*. Nashville: Discipleship Resources, 1983.

Wells, David F. *God the Evangelist*. Grand Rapids: W. B. Eerdmans, 1987.

Worley, Robert C. *Preaching and Teaching in the Earliest Church*. Philadelphia: Westminster, 1967.

Appendix

Material for the Response Guide

NOTE: It will be helpful if all or a portion of "Why a Call for Decision" accompanies your response guide. If you are using a regular bulletin fold, this data could appear inside on the left-hand page and the response portion could appear inside on the right-hand side.

Why a Call for Decision?

Many people become annoyed and frustrated when the missioner challenges them to consider important decisions in their lives. Most folks would rather be entertained or have their hearts warmed and remain basically (and comfortably) the same people they were before hearing the message.

That would be easier, but the proclamation of the good news demands a response. No person can sit idly by if he/she has *really heard* the message. The person must accept, reject, or reduce it—along with the Lord who reaches out to persons through that message.

The challenge is essential also because of your nature as a free being. God has not created you as a robot to be manipulated. The only way to enter a covenant with God or any specific aspect of the Christian life is by the free decision of your will. Therefore, I extend this response guide in His name. This guide covers the major relationships of your life—God, church, others, world, self—which comprise the possibilities of your full reconciliation in Jesus Christ.

Now, persons begin the Christian life in either of two ways: They make a basic general commitment to Christ and then work to make it specific; or they begin by making a very specific commitment to Christ and then consider making it general and total. God encourages you to begin (or continue) in the path that seems most natural to you.

Do not check anything just to be checking something or because the person sitting next to you did. This is more than a piece of paper. It represents your deepest yearnings and commitments.

My Response to the Gospel

God, being my helper, I now look carefully at these important areas of my life and make the following decision(s):

My Relationship to God

1. Tonight I consciously become a Christian. I accept God's forgiveness and acceptance of me; I deeply want to live by his will for my life and the world.   ( )
2. I rededicate myself to following Christ's lead in every area of my life.   ( )

My Relationship to the Church

3. I want to enroll in a confirmation class.   ( )
4. I want to join the _____ Church. ( )
5. I pledge my efforts for church renewal.   ( )
6. I am interested in a full-time church-related occupa-tion.   ( )
7. I desire to join a koinonia (study, sharing, action) group.   ( )

8. I want to be a caring person. ( )

My Relationship to Others

9. I will follow Christ in accepting *all* people. ( )
10. I commit myself to the Christian family. ( )
11. I will serve others in my occupation. ( )
12. I will relate as a Christian to non-human creatures. ( )

My Relationship to the World

13. I will work for social, political, and economic justice for all persons and groups. ( )
14. I commit myself to the lifetime cause of Christian peacemaking. ( )
15. I will become involved in the political process as a Christian. ( )
16. I am interested in Christian care force involvement in:
    poverty ( ), crime and penal reform ( ),
    drugs ( ), race ( ), population ( ),
    peace ( ), ecology ( ), the aging ( ),
    evangelism ( ), other _____ . ( )

Relationship to Myself

17. I will be a student of the faith. ( )
18. I will prayerfully review my giving. ( )
19. I will accept a needed discipline for my life. ( )
20. I will practice daily devotions. ( )
21. Please write down any other commitments. ( )

Name: _____

Address: _____